What people are saying

"Here at Citibank we use the Quick Course® computer tra
for 'just-in-time' job aids—the books are great for users who are too busy for
tutorials and training. Quick Course® books provide very clear instruction
and easy reference."

Bill Moreno, Development Manager
Citibank
San Francisco, CA

"At Geometric Results, much of our work is PC related and we need training
tools that can quickly and effectively improve the PC skills of our people.
Early this year we began using your materials in our internal PC training
curriculum and the results have been outstanding. Both participants and
instructors like the books and the measured learning outcomes have been very
favorable."

Roger Hill, Instructional Systems Designer
Geometric Results Incorporated
Southfield, MI

"The concise and well organized text features numbered instructions, screen
shots, and useful quick reference pointers, and tips…[This] affordable text is
very helpful for educators who wish to build proficiency."

Computer Literacy column
Curriculum Administrator Magazine
Stamford, CT

"I have purchased five other books on this subject that I've probably paid
more than $60 for, and your [Quick Course®] book taught me more than those
five books combined!"

Emory Majors
Searcy, AR

"I would like you to know how much I enjoy the Quick Course® books I have
received from you. The directions are clear and easy to follow with attention
paid to every detail of the particular lesson."

Betty Weinkauf, Retired Senior
Mission, TX

QUICK COURSE®

in

MICROSOFT®

INTERNET EXPLORER 4

ONLINE PRESS INC.

Microsoft Press

PUBLISHED BY
Microsoft Press
A Division of Microsoft Corporation
One Microsoft Way
Redmond, WA 98052-6399

Library of Congress Cataloging-in-Publication Data

Quick Course in Microsoft Internet Explorer 4 / Online Press Inc.
     p.   cm.
   Includes index.
   ISBN 1-57231-804-X
   1. Microsoft Internet Explorer   2. World Wide Web (Information retrieval system)   3. Internet (Computer network) I. Online Press Inc.
TK5105.883.M53Q53   1997
005.7'13769 - - dc21   97-31807
                                                   CIP

Printed and bound in the United States of America.

1 2 3 4 5 6 7 8 9 QMQM 3 2 1 0 9 8

Distributed to the book trade in Canada by Macmillan of Canada, a division of Canada Publishing Corporation.

A CIP record for this book is available from the British Library.

Microsoft Press books are available through booksellers and distributors worldwide. For further information about international editions, contact your local Microsoft Corporation office, or contact Microsoft Press International directly at fax (425) 936-7329. Visit our Web site at mspress.microsoft.com.

A Quick Course® Education/Training Edition for this title is published by Online Press Inc. For information about supplementary workbooks, contact Online Press Inc. at 14320 NE 21st St., Suite 18, Bellevue, WA, 98007, USA, 1-800-854-3344.

Authors: Joyce Cox, co-owner of Online Press Inc.; Ted Cox, a science teacher at Bellevue High School; and Eric Heydrick, an award-winning Webmaster. All three do their Web surfing in Bellevue, Washington.
Acquisitions Editor: Susanne M. Freet
Project Editor: Maureen Williams Zimmerman

From the publisher

"I love these books!"

I can't tell you the number of times people have said those exact words to me about our new Quick Course® software training book series. And when I ask them what makes the books so special, this is what they say:

- **They're short and approachable, but they give you hours worth of good information.**

  Written for busy people with limited time, most Quick Course books are designed to be completed in 15 to 40 hours. Because Quick Course books are usually divided into two parts—Learning the Basics and Building Proficiency—users can selectively choose the chapters that meet their needs and complete them as time allows.

- **They're relevant and fun, and they assume you're no dummy.**

  Written in an easy-to-follow, step-by-step format, Quick Course books offer streamlined instruction for the new user in the form of no-nonsense, to-the-point tutorials and learning exercises. Each book provides a logical sequence of instructions for creating useful business documents—the same documents people use on the job. People can either follow along directly or substitute their own information and customize the documents. After finishing a book, users have a valuable "library" of documents they can continually recycle and update with new information.

- **They're direct and to the point, and they're a lot more than just pretty pictures.**

  Training-oriented rather than feature-oriented, Quick Course books don't cover the things you don't really need to know to do useful work. They offer easy-to-follow, step-by-step instructions; lots of screen shots for checking work in progress; quick-reference pointers for fast, easy lookup and review; and useful tips offering additional information on topics being discussed.

- **They're a rolled-into-one-book solution, and they meet a variety of training needs.**

  Designed with instructional flexibility in mind, Quick Course books can be used both for self-training and as the basis for weeklong courses, two-day seminars, and all-day workshops. They can be adapted to meet a variety of training needs, including classroom instruction, take-away practice exercises, and self-paced learning.

Microsoft Press is very excited about bringing you this extraordinary series. But you must be the judge. I hope you'll give these books a try. And maybe the next time I see you, you too will say, "Hey, Jim! I love these books!"

Jim Brown, Publisher
Microsoft Press

Content overview

Content details

Introduction

This book is a fast-paced introduction to using Microsoft Internet Explorer 4. In the first chapter, we introduce the program, show you how to use the updated Windows desktop, talk a bit about intranets, and then take a look at the part of the Internet known as the World Wide Web. In Chapter 2, we take a tour of the Internet Start page, and you learn how to search for information and how to easily download files with FTP. In Chapter 3, we show you how to customize Internet Explorer. Next, two chapters discuss communicating over the Internet, first with electronic mail (called *e-mail* from now on) and then with a variety of new Internet Explorer tools that are part of Microsoft NetMeeting. Also included is a discussion of how to create your own Web pages to communicate with your colleagues or the world at large. Finally, in Chapter 6 we show you how to participate in newsgroups, where people with similar interests exchange information.

The Internet is huge and far-reaching and its resources are so vast that it's easy to waste a lot of time if we don't know what we're doing. So instead of simply leading you from one nifty place to another, we show you techniques for using Internet Explorer to access Internet resources efficiently. (Of course, if you are paying for your own Internet account and you want to try your hand at "surfing the Net," feel free to explore all the interesting tangents you are bound to discover as you work your way through this book. Those of you who are taking this tour on someone else's nickel will want to check with the powers-that-be before using your work time for such surfing safaris, all the while running up hourly connect charges or monopolizing the resources of the computer that provides your access to the Internet.)

There's no such thing as free Internet access

People who access the Internet through corporate, government, or educational servers are often under the illusion that their Internet access is free. Although they may not have to pay for access out of their own pockets, *someone* is footing the bill for the computer resources and technology (fiber optic cable, satellites, and other communications gizmos) needed to make everything work. In the early days, Internet development was funded by government and public education agencies—in other words, by taxpayers like you and me. Now corporations and fee-paying users share the burden with these agencies, but the agencies still have to provide for Internet support in their tax-supported budgets.

What Do We Need to Use This Book?

We wrote this book using Internet Explorer 4 on computers running Windows 95 and Windows NT Workstation 4. We found only minor differences between them as far as Internet Explorer's operation is concerned. All our screen graphics are from Windows 95, but if you are running Windows NT you will have no difficulty following along.

We assume that the full version of Internet Explorer 4 is already installed on your computer and that you are ready to go. We don't cover all the ins and outs of choosing an Internet service provider (ISP) and configuring your system to make the necessary connections because many of you will have no choice about your avenue of access to the Internet. If you are using this book in conjunction with an instructor-led course, your instructor has already set up your learning environment using whatever Internet connection is available. Similarly, if you are using this book to teach yourself how to access the Internet from your computer at work, your supervisor or network administrator will already have set up your account and provided instructions for making the connection. If you want to access the Internet from your own computer, see the adjacent tip for hints about how to set up an Internet account.

Microsoft may issue upgrades to Internet Explorer from time to time, and the Web site you see when you start the program is updated frequently. What's more, the Internet itself is in a constant state of flux. So one thing you'll need as you work your way through this book is *flexibility*. For our examples, we have tried to select the more stable areas of the Internet, but even they are subject to change. So don't get uptight if your screen doesn't look exactly the same as ours. Change is a fact of life on the Internet, and staying flexible is the best way to cope with it.

The only other thing you'll need as you follow the instructions in this book is *common sense*. The growth in public interest in the Internet has been accompanied by a lot of media hype about the dangers of falling victim to a rip-off artist or a hacker, or of stumbling across unsavory information or unsavory characters. Let's put this hype in perspective.

Individual Internet access

One of the easiest ways to get hooked up to the Internet is to subscribe to an online service that provides Internet access, such as America Online (AOL) or The Microsoft Network (MSN). When you first click The Internet icon on your desktop, a setup wizard kindly offers to help you connect using one of these services. Alternatively, you can open an account with a local company that provides Internet access. To track down a local Internet service provider (ISP), check advertisements in local newspapers. (A free weekly paper called *Computer User* is a good source if it is published in your area.) Before you sign on with any provider, check that you can use Internet Explorer 4 as your browser and ask for information about setting things up. Later on, if you are dissatisfied with your ISP and thinking of making a switch, you can check the Web sites at *www.thelist.com* or *www.boardwatch.com* to find all the ISPs in your area.

How Safe Is the Internet?

Well, it depends what we mean by *safe*. Usually people who ask this question have concerns that fall into one or more of the categories discussed below.

Information Security

The primary concern here is the confidentiality of personal and financial information, such as credit card numbers. When we send information across the Internet, it is routed from one computer to another depending on current traffic patterns until it reaches its final destination. Potentially, any computer along this unpredictable route can copy the information, and any criminally inclined person with access to that computer can then make use of it. Efforts are ongoing to create secure Web sites for buying and selling and transferring confidential information, but it is up to us to exercise a little caution. Secure sites—those that encrypt information so that it cannot be hijacked in a readable form while it is in transit—are identified in Internet Explorer's status bar by a lock icon. If we don't see this icon, common sense says we shouldn't send out personal or financial information that we'd rather keep private. Internet Explorer provides a variety of features to help us protect both our wallets and our privacy and by default, displays a warning when we are about to send information to an unsecure site. See page 91 for more information about ways to protect against security leaks.

Credit cards

Secure sites

A secondary concern is the issue of system snooping and other activities of programs known as *cookies*. When we visit some Web sites, the site transfers a tiny cookie file to our hard drive that collects information about our identity and about what we did when we visited the site. If we return later, the site checks the cookie file to learn what we did during the last visit. Potentially, the site can use the cookie file to build a user profile that is valuable for targeted advertising. If you don't like the idea of this sort of information gathering, you can have Internet Explorer warn you when a cookie is about to be transferred to your computer or block the transfer entirely; see page 92 for more information.

Cookies

System Security

Viruses

The concerns here fall into two categories: viruses and uninvited tampering. We can't "catch" a virus by looking at information on the Internet. But if we download an infected program from the Internet and then run that program, we can end up with a very sick computer. Common sense says that if we want to acquire some of the goodies available on the Internet without becoming a victim of germ warfare, we should set up a system for checking our acquisitions before doing anything with them. Unfortunately, most people don't bother to set up such a system until *after* they are laid low by their first infection. Take it from someone who knows: viruses are not to be sneezed at. We urge you to invest in virus scanning software and follow the simple strategy on page 55 so that you can safely use the Internet's resources.

Another way to prevent rogue programs from damaging your computer is to take advantage of Internet Explorer's security features designed to block programs from unknown sources while allowing you to accept ones from trusted sources (see page 114). Until you have had a chance to investigate these features, our advice is to always abort any action for which Internet Explorer displays a warning message.

Push and pull technologies

The concern about uninvited tampering stems from misunderstandings about *push* technology. Web browsing has traditionally been *pull* technology; nothing appeared on our screen unless we pulled it off the Web. With push technology, Web sites don't wait for us to come looking; they actively push their material at us. But here's the thing: they can't push anything in our direction unless we *ask* them to, by *subscribing* to their sites or services. We show you how to subscribe on page 106, but in the meantime, you can rest easy.

Sleaze

Perhaps the most hyped-up danger of the Internet is that of coming face-to-face with the seedy side of life. There is no question that this possibility exists. However, in countless hours of working on the Internet, we have yet to experience this problem. On a few occasions where a sloppy search request produced listings that we could readily identify as sleaze, we simply avoided displaying the material. And we have deliberately steered clear of Web sites, e-mail messages, and newsgroups that we suspected might carry material we would find embarrassing or offensive. Common sense says that censoring the Internet not only flies in the face of the right to free speech but is also impossible given the Internet's global reach. Common sense also says that if we are concerned about sleaze on the Internet, we should use the filtering capabilities included in Internet Explorer or those of off-the-shelf filtering programs (such as CyberPatrol) to block the display of this type of information. On page 116, we show you how to use Internet Explorer's Content Advisor to prevent materials with specified language, nudity, sex, and violence ratings from being viewed on your computer.

Filtering capabilities

Sleazy People

Even with cookies and push technology, browsing the Internet is usually a one-way process. A Web site might count the number of people who visit it, but unless we specifically fill out a questionnaire with personal information or allow cookies to be transferred to our computer, no one knows exactly who the visitors are. Sending e-mail and participating in newsgroups are two-way, interactive processes, and as with all interactions between human beings, they can bring us into contact with low-life characters we would ordinarily avoid. By definition, these people don't have our best interests at heart, and they may even derive some kinky pleasure out of doing us harm. So common sense says that because we have no way of really knowing the people at the other end of e-mail messages or newsgroup articles, we should never divulge personal information such as address, phone number, or age. Internet Explorer can't help us with this one; it's up to us.

Like society in general, the Internet certainly has its criminal element, its red-light district, and its deviants. But as we've said, with a little common sense, we can take advantage of the huge positive part of the Internet without bumping into the very small negative part. It is that positive part that we'll explore in the following chapters, but if you run into any security-related message boxes while you are exploring on your own, you will probably want to err on the side of caution and cancel the action that prompted the message until you've worked your way through this book.

CAUTION

ONE

LEARNING THE BASICS

In Part One, we cover basic techniques for working with Internet Explorer 4. After you complete these three chapters, you'll know enough to be able to use the Internet to find information and send e-mail. In Chapter 1, you learn some Internet concepts, explore Internet Explorer's new interface, and take a short trip on the World Wide Web. In Chapter 2, you see how to find information on the Web and how to download files using FTP. In Chapter 3, you learn the ins and outs of e-mail using Outlook Express, which comes with Internet Explorer.

1

Introducing
Internet Explorer 4

We start with definitions of a few key terms, take a look at the Internet Explorer 4 interface, and then fire up the program for a quick jaunt on the World Wide Web. You learn how to move around and what URLs are all about.

Use Web-style navigation buttons in My Computer

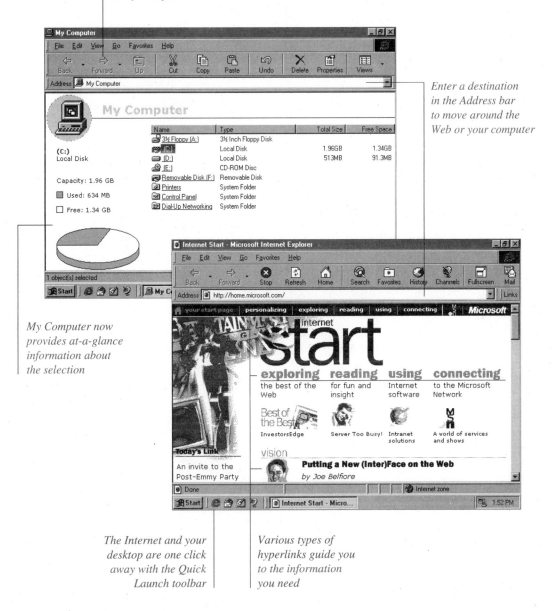

Enter a destination in the Address bar to move around the Web or your computer

My Computer now provides at-a-glance information about the selection

The Internet and your desktop are one click away with the Quick Launch toolbar

Various types of hyperlinks guide you to the information you need

Most books about the Internet assume you need a ton of background information before you can start exploring. Because we don't have to cover making connections and so forth, we can give you a few ounces of information and then jump right in.

Getting Oriented

In a few minutes, we'll fire up Internet Explorer, but we need to make sure we are all speaking the same language before we take the plunge. We promise to keep this short.

- **The Internet.** A contraction of *inter-networks* (or *between networks*). Started in the 60s as a connection between Department of Defense computers at four sites across the US, the Internet now connects millions of computers all over the world. Nobody "owns" the Internet, and nobody has overall management responsibility. Government agencies, universities, research establishments, and corporate entities own their particular network of computers and decide whether those computers will be connected to the Internet, who will be allowed to access them, and for what purpose. Anarchy is held at bay because the Internet is perceived as useful, and everyone cooperates to make it work. But other than broad rules governing connection technicalities and some even broader rules governing Internet behavior, everyone pretty much does his or her own thing. As a result, the Internet was used for years by only those experts who could navigate its maze of resources and deal with its mess of inconsistencies by typing cryptic commands.

- **Cyberspace.** Not a *thing*, but a *concept* first postulated by William Gibson in 1984 in his science-fiction novel *Neuromancer*. Cyberspace now refers to all the communication and other interaction that happens on the Internet. We can think of cyberspace as a global culture or society that is evolving its own language, customs, and other badges of membership.

- **The World Wide Web.** Invented by Tim Berners-Lee in 1989 in Switzerland, the Web is a special part of the Internet. Like the Internet, it's not a *thing*. It's a connection that allows

Internet II

The popularity of the Web has resulted in major connectivity problems for the agencies and institutions it was designed to assist. One possible solution to this "bandwidth bog-down" is being referred to as *Internet II*. Expected to take at least three years to put into place, Internet II is intended to serve scientists and scholars at research universities and high-tech companies. Whether this newer, faster service will ever be available to the general public remains to be decided.

people to view information stored on participating computers. The difference is that Web information is governed by a much tighter set of rules than information on the rest of the Internet. These rules specify how the text, graphics, and other elements that make up the information should be formatted, so that information on one computer can be linked to information on another computer in a potentially infinite "web." The rules also mean that Web information is more consistent, making accessing the information easier for beginning and intermediate Internet users.

- **Web sites.** Information resources published on the Web by government agencies, companies, organizations, and individuals. Each site has an address called a *universal resource locator* (*URL*) that identifies the computer on which the files that make up the site's information are stored (see page 22 for more information). These files can consist of text, graphics, and multimedia components such as audio and video clips, all coded in such a way that they can be viewed by programs called *Web browsers* (see page 6). Web sites can also include mini-programs written in the Java language (see the tip on page 33 for more information about Java). Usually, the information stored at each Web site is divided into easily viewed chunks called *pages*, and the starting point of each Web site is its *home page*. We can jump from one page to another, both within a single Web site and between Web sites, by clicking *hyperlinks*, which appear on the screen as specially formatted text (usually a different color and underlined) or as graphics. (Don't worry if you're confused right now; all these terms will fall into place when you actually start moving around a Web site.)

Universal resource locators (URLs)

Web pages

Hyperlinks

- **Internet service providers (ISPs).** Organizations that own the computers through which we access the Internet. Government agencies, educational institutions, and large corporations generally have computers that are directly connected to the Internet, and they control access for their individual members, students, or employees. The simplest way for small organizations and individuals to gain access is to use a modem to connect their computer to the computer of a commercial service that provides access for a fee. The term *Internet service provider* refers, in its narrowest sense, to this type of service and includes online information services such as The Microsoft Network (MSN) and America Online (AOL), as well as companies whose sole business is to provide Internet access. However, for simplicity we use the term *Internet service provider* in this book to refer to all avenues of access—whether we receive a bill or not.

- **Intranets.** Private Web look-alikes. Using Internet technology, many companies are setting up Internet servers and creating intranets that are accessible only from the company's computers (no matter where they are physically located). Intranets enable people to easily and cheaply access company information, exchange ideas, and collaborate on projects. A system of security "firewalls" ensures that intranet information is available only to the people in the company who are authorized to access it, not to general Internet users. See page 16 for a brief discussion of intranets.

- **Web browsers.** Programs we run on our computer so that we can view information stored on the World Wide Web. The browser interprets the information, displays it on the screen, and enables us to move between linked items. The first Web browsers, such as Mosaic, were developed on university campuses and were distributed for free. Since then, commercial companies have gotten in on the act, developing increasingly sophisticated browsers. As the browsers get fancier, so does the information available for viewing on the Web, to the point where high-ticket marketing companies are now in the business of designing Web sites that are as compelling as many television commercials. As you already know, this book is about the Internet Explorer Web browser.

Well that's it for the definitions for now. With that common understanding of what we are working with, let's talk about Internet Explorer.

Extranets

Some companies are taking the concept of intranets one step further and are developing hybrid sites that allow outsiders, such as vendors and distributors, limited access to material stored on company intranets. Called *extranets*, these sites provide cost-effective, timely information to authorized people both inside and outside the company, while keeping the information secure from broader access.

The New Internet Explorer 4 Interface

When you turn on your computer after installing Internet Explorer 4, the desktop looks like this:

Big deal, huh? But looks can be deceiving. Behind the scenes, Internet Explorer has revamped the Windows interface so that it can function like a Web page. You'll have a better understanding of what this means by the time you have finished this chapter, but we want to point out some of the changes now so that you know what to expect when you are carrying out everyday computer tasks.

When Internet Explorer 4 was installed on your computer, you were asked whether you wanted to install the Windows Desktop Update. We assume you clicked Yes to copy the update files to your hard drive; see the tip on page 8 if you need to install the Windows Desktop Update now. We also assume you know how to start programs, work with tools such as My Computer, and otherwise manipulate objects on the Windows 95/NT desktop; if you don't, you might want to check out *Quick Course in Windows 95* or *Quick Course in Windows NT Workstation 4*, two books in the Quick Course series that will help you come up to speed. Here, we want to

NT Service Pack 3

To use Internet Explorer 4 on a computer running Windows NT Workstation 4, you must have Service Pack 3 installed. Microsoft releases service packs from time to time to update the operating system (fix bugs and patch security holes) and improve performance. You can download Service Pack 3 from Microsoft's Web site (*www.microsoft.com*) or you can order it on CD-ROM by calling (800) 426-9400.

see how the desktop behaves when it has a Web-like interface. Follow these steps:

1. If necessary, start your computer. The first time you start your computer after installing Internet Explorer, you see a Welcome window like this one:

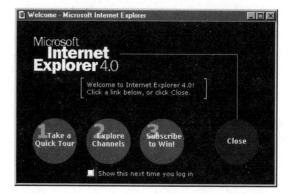

2. If you want to be able to check out the blue circles later, click the Show This Next Time You Log In check box; otherwise, leave it unchecked. Then click the red Close circle to close the window. Your screen then looks something like the one shown on the previous page.

Don't worry if your desktop looks different from ours. For one thing, you may have a larger monitor. But quite apart from that, one of the hallmarks of Windows 95/NT is the way you can set up your desktop to suit the way you work (or your company can set it up to suit the way it wants you to work). In the first column on the left of our desktop are the familiar icons for My Computer, Network Neighborhood, Recycle Bin, and My Briefcase, as well as a shortcut icon for Windows Explorer. In the second column are icons pertaining to Internet communications. The shortcut to Northwest Nexus is our Dial-Up Networking connection to our ISP. You may see an icon representing your avenue of access to the Internet, or access may be controlled by another computer on your network. The big *e* represents Internet Explorer (you're going to see this icon everywhere). The other two icons represent the e-mail services available on our machine (Outlook Express

Installing Windows Desktop Update

To install the Windows Desktop Update, connect to your ISP. Then click the Start button on the taskbar, point to Settings, and click Control Panel. Double-click Add/Remove Programs, then click Microsoft Internet Explorer 4.0, and click Add/Remove. Then click Add Windows Desktop Update From Web Site and follow instructions.

and Microsoft Exchange). If you use a different e-mail program, you may see its icon on your desktop.

Let's go exploring:

1. Point to the Internet Explorer icon. This description pops up: ◄──────────────────

Desktop descriptions

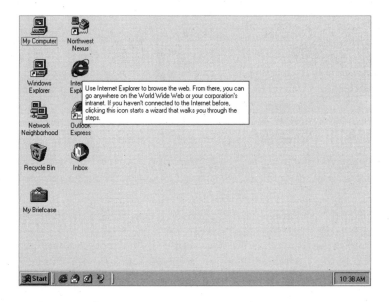

2. Point to some of the other icons and read their pop-up descriptions if they have them.

3. Double-click the My Computer icon as you usually would to open its window.

   At this point, your computer could respond in one of several ways, and we need to get everyone in sync for the rest of the section. Follow these steps:

1. You may see a dialog box telling you that you have the option ◄──────────────────
   of single-clicking items instead of double-clicking them. If
   you select the single-click option, you can treat items on your
   desktop the same way you treat them on a Web page (called
   Web style), or you can treat items on your desktop the way you
   always have (called *Classic style*). To try the new approach,
   select Single-Click and click OK.

Single-clicking vs.
double-clicking

2. Whether you see the dialog box or not, check your settings by choosing Folder Options from My Computer's View menu to display this dialog box:

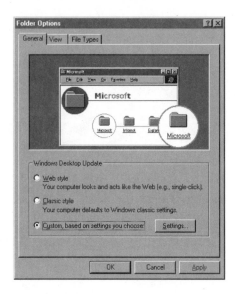

3. Click the Custom, Based On Settings You Choose option to select it, then click the Settings button to display the dialog box pictured below:

Initial capital letters

In this book, you'll notice that sometimes the option names we use don't exactly match those you see on the screen. We always capitalize the first letter of every word so that you won't stumble when you see the option names in a sentence. For example, in step 3 we tell you to click the Custom, Based On Settings You Choose option, when the option name on the screen is Custom, based on settings you choose. See what we mean? When all the words start with a capital letter, they stand out better, don't they?

4. Check that all your settings are the same as ours, click OK twice to close the dialog boxes, and then close My Computer.

Back on the desktop, all your icon names are now underlined. (They may have been all along, but now you know that your settings are the same as ours, so you'll have no surprises.)

Now let's try out Web style. To keep our commentary to a minimum, we'll avoid pointing out the obvious, but notice the subtle and not-so-subtle changes on the screen as you follow along with these steps:

1. Move the pointer over the My Computer icon, noticing that the pointer changes to a hand and the icon's name changes color to indicate that it is selected.

2. Click the icon to open the My Computer window, which looks like this:

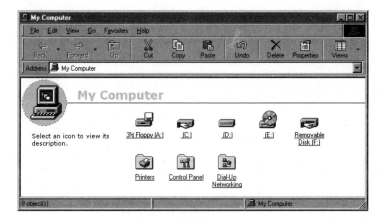

(We've enlarged the window so you can see all its contents.) The impact of Internet Explorer is very apparent in the My Computer window. Go and Favorites menus have been added to the menu bar (you'll learn how to use the Favorites menu on page 46); the buttons on the toolbar have a new look; the old Look In box has become its own Address bar; and the information in the list box is presented in a new way. These changes are typical of those you'll find in other places, such as Windows Explorer and Control Panel.

3. Point to the (C:) icon in the My Computer window to select the drive. Then maximize the window so that it looks like the one on the next page.

New toolbars

To the right of the Start button on the taskbar, you see a new Quick Launch toolbar with buttons for quickly moving to the Internet. Also available for display on the taskbar are the Address, Links, and Desktop toolbars; see page 110 for more information.

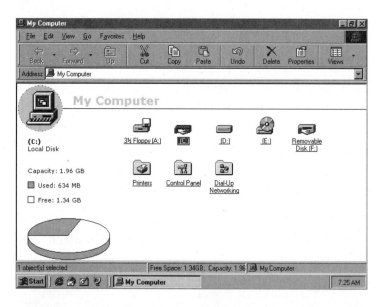

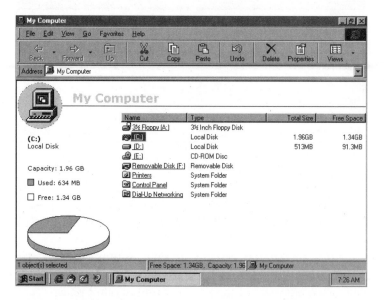

The Views button

4. Click the arrow to the right of the Views button on the toolbar and select Details from the drop-down list. Here's the result:

The Up button

5. Click the (C:) icon to display its contents, and then click the Up button on the toolbar to move up one folder level to the My Computer window. Notice that changing the view in one window does not affect the view in other windows.

6. Click the Back button to move to the previously displayed folder window. Notice that the Forward button is now active.

The Back and Forward buttons

7. Experiment with using the buttons to move around, finishing up with the (C:) window displayed. Then click the Windows folder icon to open its window.

8. Scroll the list box to display the first file icon (after all the folders) and point to the first file icon to select it. Hold down the Shift key, move the pointer over to the third file icon, release the Shift key, and move the pointer to a blank area of the screen. All three files are now selected.

9. Now hold down the Ctrl key, point to the third file icon, release the Ctrl key, and move the pointer to a blank area. Here's the result:

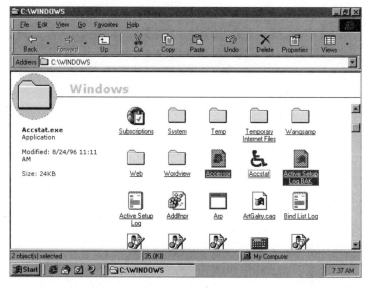

10. Click the arrow to the right of the Back button and select My Computer from the drop-down list, or click the Up button until you arrive at the My Computer window.

Once you have selected a file or folder, you can move, copy, or delete it in the usual way (but don't try this with the files and folders in the Windows folder or you will almost certainly mess up your system).

Want the same view in all folder windows?

If you prefer a particular view, you can tell Internet Explorer to set folder windows to that view unless you change it. Choose Folder Options from the View menu, click the View tab, select the Like Current Folder option, and click OK. If you've changed the view for a few folders and you now want all folder windows to have the default view, select the Reset All Folders option in this dialog box.

Bringing the Web to the Desktop

My Computer's View menu now includes commands that are designed to put the resources of the Internet or a company intranet at our fingertips from wherever we are currently working. Follow these steps to try some of these commands:

1. Choose Toolbars and then Links from the View menu. The Links toolbar joins the Standard toolbar and the Address bar at the top of the window. (If your Links toolbar appears to the right of one of the other bars, see the tip below.) The bars at the top of the window should look like this:

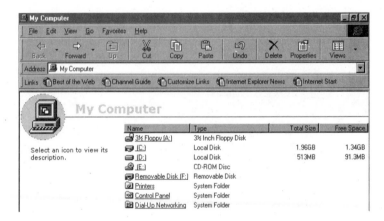

2. Run the pointer slowly over the buttons on the Links toolbar and notice that the description boxes that pop up contain strings of apparent gibberish. These strings are Web addresses, known as *URLs* (see page 22), which allow you to jump directly to a specific Web site from My Computer simply by clicking a button. (If you click one of these buttons while you're not connected to the Internet, one or more dialog boxes may appear. For now, close the dialog boxes without making any changes and selecting the option to stay unconnected, which is called *working offline*.)

Moving toolbars

You can move the toolbars around to come up with a configuration that suits the way you work. If your Links toolbar doesn't look like the one in our screen, point to the word *Links*, hold down the left mouse button, and when the pointer changes to crossed arrows, drag down and over to the left. The toolbar will pop into place below the Address bar.

3. Choose Explorer Bar and then Channels from the View menu. (Again, if you see a message box prompting you to connect, continue working offline.) The list-box area now splits into two panes to display the Explorer bar on the left, with the Microsoft Channel Guide displayed in it, as shown here:

We explain channels on page 108. The idea here is to show you yet another way in which Internet Explorer makes a seamless connection between your daily work and the Web.

4. Choose other commands from the Explorer Bar submenu, finishing up with None, which closes the bar.

Reverting to the Traditional Display

After this little taste of Internet Explorer's impact on tools such as My Computer, you may decide you would rather wait until you've finished this book to get used to the changes. For a temporary fix, we can switch the list box of a particular folder window to a traditional display without affecting any other windows. Follow these steps:

1. Choose As Web Page from the View menu to toggle off this command. The window now displays only the contents of My Computer, without the header and the additional information.

2. Click the (C:) icon. Its window still displays its contents as a Web page.

We can change all windows to a traditional display and switch back to double-clicking using the steps on the next page.

The Active Desktop

When you have installed the Windows Desktop Update, you can turn on the Active Desktop interface by right-clicking a blank area of the desktop and choosing Active Desktop and then View As Web Page from the object menu. You can then place items from Web pages directly on your desktop and, provided you are connected to the Internet, the items will be constantly updated from their source Web pages. See page 111 for more information about customizing your desktop with active Web items.

1. Choose Folder Options from the View menu to display the dialog box shown earlier on page 10.

2. Click the Classic Style option and then click OK. (This change may not take effect right away. If necessary, close My Computer and then open it again to confirm that you can now move around traditional folder windows in double-click fashion.)

3. Close My Computer.

A Word About Intranets

Companies and institutions are increasingly installing intranets to distribute information in a more efficient manner than is possible using paper. If your organization has an intranet, your system administrator may have created a configuration file that automatically sets up Internet Explorer on your computer to access the intranet. To implement the settings in this file, follow these steps:

The Internet Explorer icon

1. Double-click the Internet Explorer icon to start the program.

2. Choose Internet Options from the View menu and click the Connection tab. Click the Configure button in the Automatic Configuration section, type the path of the file in the URL box (your system administrator will give you this information), and click OK.

The Refresh button

3. Click the Refresh button on the toolbar to put the file's setting into effect.

From then on, your intranet's home page will automatically be loaded when you start Internet Explorer and you can apply the navigation techniques you learn in this chapter to your intranet's Web pages.

A Look at the Web

Quick Course books usually keep to a minimum the amount of reading you have to do at any one time and take a "learn by doing" approach to teaching software. We'll try to stick to that model as much as possible. But here's a hint: so that you are not sitting reading explanations while time is ticking away on your Internet account, you might want to take the time to read the text sections ahead of time. Then when you're ready, rejoin us for our first look at the World Wide Web.

Starting Internet Explorer

When you start Internet Explorer for this example, you will probably be asked to enter an account name and password so that you can identify yourself to your ISP and gain access to the Internet. The exact procedure varies from provider to provider. In the steps below, we follow the procedure for accessing the Internet using a Dial-Up Networking connection to our ISP. You should simply substitute the procedure for your own ISP or your network. Here goes:

1. Connect to your ISP.

2. Double-click the Internet Explorer icon on your desktop to start the program. After some initial screen activity, Internet Explorer displays the Internet Start page provided by Microsoft, which looks something like this:

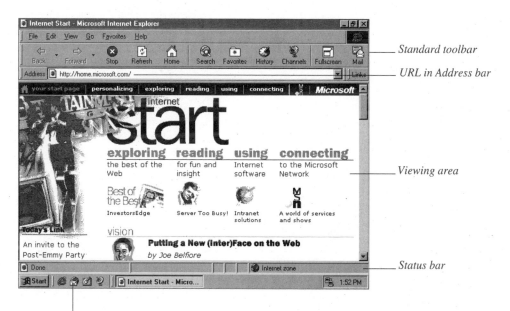

Standard toolbar

URL in Address bar

Viewing area

Status bar

Quick Launch toolbar

(We've moved the links toolbar to the right of the Address bar to enlarge the viewing area; see the tip on page 14.)

If displaying this page takes a while, don't be concerned. This site is accessed millions of times a day, and even with the fastest modem, access can be slow at peak traffic times.

Moving to Another Web Site

We'll come back to this screen in Chapter 2 and use some of the tools it provides for navigating the Web, but for now let's take a look at the Quick Course Web site. (This is not a feeble attempt at self-promotion. Because Web sites come and go and change so often, sending you to our own site is the best way for us to know exactly what you are going to see as you move around. Once you are familiar with how Web sites work, we won't worry so much that you'll get disoriented if the site has changed since we wrote this book.) Follow these steps to move to a different site:

1. Click the URL in the Address box to select it.

2. Now type *www,* then a period, then *quickcourse.com.* Check that the entire entry now reads *www.quickcourse.com* and press Enter. Because the URL begins with *www,* Internet Explorer adds *http://* in front of it. (You have to type *http://* for URLs that don't begin with *www.*) After a flurry of activity, Internet Explorer displays this Quick Course home page:

More about the Address bar

The Address bar is a very versatile component of the Internet Explorer interface. You can move it, size it, browse folders and run programs from it, and use it to search the Internet. See page 98 for more information.

Moving Around a Web Site

As you'll see, reading the information at a Web site is not at all like reading a book. Follow these steps to get a feel for how Web information is organized and how to move around a Web site:

1. Move the pointer over the row of graphics below the title, noticing as you go that the pointer changes to a hand to indicate that the graphics are hyperlinks. (Don't click anything yet.)

2. Scroll through the home page using the scroll bar, and move the pointer over the text on the page, noticing how the pointer changes to a hand over underlined words to show that they are text hyperlinks.

3. Scroll to the top of the home page, point to the *Catalog* graphic hyperlink, and when the pointer changes to a hand, click the left mouse button. Your screen now looks like this:

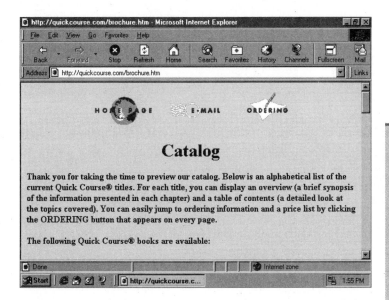

Problems connecting to a Web site

If you see a message like *Internet Explorer cannot open the Internet site http://www.quickcourse.com/*, check to make sure you haven't typed an extra period, misspelled a word, or otherwise entered the URL incorrectly. The message might also mean that the site's server is overloaded. Increasingly busy sites pose a common obstacle to Web connections. If you know you've typed the URL correctly, you might want to try that site again later.

4. Scroll the list of titles until you see *Quick Course in Office 97*, and then click the *Overview* text hyperlink. Turn the page to see the result.

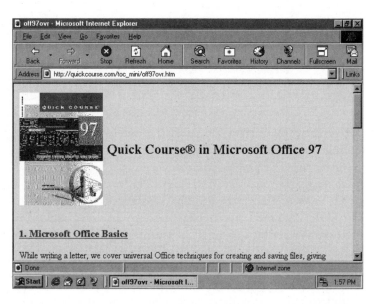

Suppose we want to go back to the title list to check out a different book. The Back and Forward buttons that we saw earlier on the My Computer toolbar also appear on Internet Explorer's toolbar, so we can move backward and forward through the pages we have already displayed, no matter which Web site those pages belong to. Try this:

1. Click the Back button to redisplay the catalog page, then click Back again to redisplay the home page.

Hyperlinks you've already viewed

2. Click the Forward button to redisplay the catalog page. Notice that the Overview hyperlink for the *Quick Course in Office 97* title has changed color to remind you that you have already viewed the information on that page.

3. Scroll to *Quick Course in Windows NT Workstation 4*, and click its *Overview* hyperlink.

Some Web pages provide hyperlinks we can use to move directly from one part of the site to another. Check this out:

Jumping directly to the home page

1. Scroll to the bottom of the Windows NT overview page and click the *Home Page* graphic to move directly back to the Quick Course home page, the first page of this Web site. (Most well-designed sites include a hyperlink back to the home page from all the other pages in the site.)

2. Scroll the home page and click the *great comments* text hyperlink to display this page:

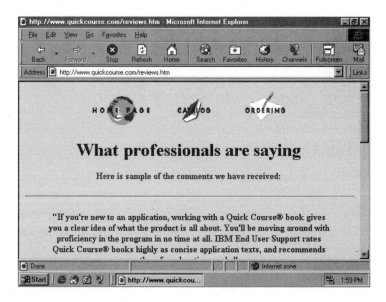

3. Click the Back button. (Clicking the *Reviews* graphic hyperlink at the top of the home page takes you to the same page
as the *great comments* text hyperlink.)

4. Click the *frequently asked questions* hyperlink, and then click
the second question, *Can you tell me something about Online
Press?* This is what you see:

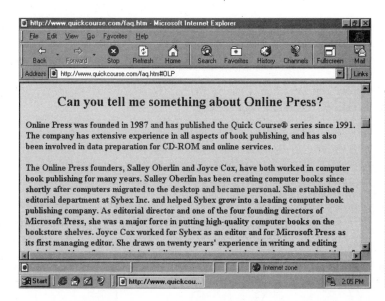

Frequently asked questions (FAQs)

So many Web sites include a frequently asked questions page that
these pages have become known
as *FAQs*. Clicking a hyperlink la-
beled FAQ takes us to the list of
questions and answers, and this is
a good place to start when we are
looking for information at a Web
site we haven't visited before.

The Home button

5. Click the Back button and then scroll the page. Notice that the page contains the list of questions at the top, followed by the answers. The hyperlinks we used previously all jumped to a linked file (a different page) that is stored at the same Web site, whereas each question hyperlink jumps to a linked place within the same file (the same page).

6. Continue testing the hyperlinks at the Quick Course Web site until you can move around with ease, and then click the Home button on the toolbar to display the Internet Start page, shown earlier on page 17.

7. If you have been collecting the addresses of Web sites you want to check out, enter one of them in the Address box and explore another Web site now. (Remember, if you get lost, click the Home button to come back to familiar territory.)

Quitting Internet Explorer

When it's time to end an Internet session, the procedure we use will depend on our ISP. In our case, quitting Internet Explorer leaves us still connected to our ISP, so quitting the program and logging off our account are two separate procedures. In the following steps, substitute whatever procedure is appropriate for your setup:

1. Click the Close button at the right end of the Internet Explorer title bar (the X) to quit the program.

2. Right-click the modem icon at the right end of the taskbar and choose Disconnect, or choose the command that signs you out of your Internet account.

Understanding URLs

We have just done a little exploring by entering the URL of a Web site in Internet Explorer's Address box. Understanding how URLs are constructed can help us keep track of where we are on the Web and can also give us some insight into how Web pages are linked. Let's go over a bit of background information before we go online again.

A few interesting sites

Here are URLs for a few other sites you might want to explore:

http://www.exploratorium.edu
The Exploratorium, a collection of news and resources related to science

http://www.intellicast.com/weather/usa
USA Weather, which gives the latest weather information for the United States

http://www.women.com
Women's Wire, which includes informative articles about women in business and entertainment

In the previous section, we displayed the Quick Course Web site by entering the following URL in the Address box:

http://www.quickcourse.com

As we showed you, Web sites like this one are constructed of pages that are connected by hyperlinks. *Hypertext* files have text links, and *hypermedia* files have text links plus other types of links such as graphics, sound, and video links. (See the tip on page 30 for information about the origin of the term *Hypertext*.)

We can jump from page to page because the people who publish Web information follow a set of rules called a *protocol*. The particular protocol used on the Web is the *HyperText Transfer Protocol* (or *HTTP*). So the first element of this URL tells Internet Explorer that we want to look at a Web resource. The resource is separated from the rest of the URL by a colon and two forward slashes.

The HTTP protocol

Next Internet Explorer needs to know the name of the computer, called the *server*, on which the Web resource is stored. This name, called the *domain name*, is a string of identifiers separated by periods. (If we have to say a domain name out loud, we call a period a *dot*, as in *www dot quickcourse dot com*.) The domain names of servers located in the US end in one of the following, which identify the type of domain:

Domain names

com	*Business organization*
edu	*Educational institution*
gov	*Government agency*
mil	*Military agency*
net	*Network administration support*
org	*Other type of organization*

(Because domain names are in increasingly short supply, the powers-that-be are trying to add new suffixes to this list.)

Other types of resources

As you'll learn in later chapters of this book, other types of resources are also available on the Internet, including the *mail*, *news*, *FTP*, *Gopher*, *WAIS*, and *telnet* resources.

The domain name might also end in a two-letter code that identifies the country where the server lives.

When we clicked the *Catalog* hyperlink at the Quick Course Web site, we jumped to a page stored on the site's server as brochure.htm. The URL in the Address box changed to this:

http://www.quickcourse.com/brochure.htm

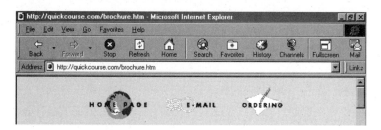

Paths in URLs

Here the domain name is followed by a single forward slash and the *path* of the file specified by the hyperlink. The path tells precisely where on the server the file is located. In this case, the path is simply the name of the file, but it could also include folders and subfolders (directories and subdirectories), all separated by single forward slashes.

Why do we need to know all this? Can't we just click our way around using the simple techniques demonstrated earlier? Of course we can. But as you'll discover when you start searching the Web on your own, some Web sites are huge collections of files in which we can explore endless mazes of information. If we get lost or want to quickly retrace our footsteps without leaving the Web site altogether, it's helpful if we have made a mental note of the site's key URLs so that we can quickly jump back to familiar pages. Let's put our new knowledge of URLs to the test:

The Launch Internet Explorer Browser button

1. Fire up your Internet connection and then start Internet Explorer, this time by clicking the Launch Internet Explorer Browser button on the Quick Launch toolbar on the taskbar.

2. With the Internet Start page displayed on your screen, replace the URL in the Address box with *www.city.net* and press Enter. Internet Explorer finds the specified Web site and displays the City.Net home page shown here:

Again, don't worry if this Web site has changed since we captured the screen pictured above.

3. Scroll down the page to the Regions section, move the pointer over the *North America* hyperlink, and check the status bar, which tells you the URL of the linked page.

4. Click the *North America* hyperlink and watch the status bar as Internet Explorer finds and opens this Web page, which is located at *http://www.city.net/regions/north_america/*:

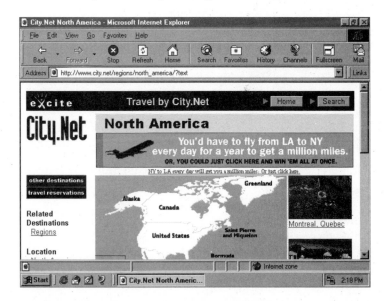

5. Point to the United States on the map of North America and click to display a map of the United States.

6. Click *Conn.* (for *Connecticut*) on the map, then click Stamford, then click *Maps*.

7. Suppose this line of investigation is not yielding the information you need. Click the URL in the Address box to select it, press End to move the insertion point to the end of the URL, backspace to remove *connecticut/stamford/maps/,* and press Enter. Internet Explorer redisplays the map of the United States, and you can take another route through the site's information.

Here's another way to jump back to a previously displayed Web page:

The History button

1. Click History on the toolbar to open the Explorer bar and display this list of all the places you have visited in this session:

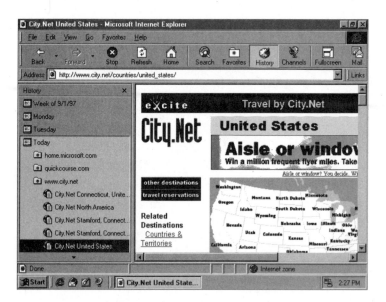

You could backtrack by selecting a site from this list, but here's another way:

2. Click the History button to close the Explorer bar, and then click the arrow to the right of the Address box to display a list of the sites you have visited:

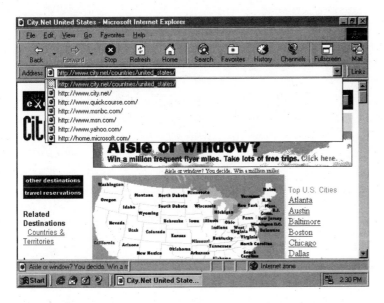

3. Choose *http://www.city.net/* from the list to jump directly to the City.Net home page.

4. If you want, explore this Web site some more. Then quit Internet Explorer and disconnect from your ISP.

   Well, that's it for the quick tour. In the next chapter, we'll feature more ways of exploring the Web.

2

Finding Information on the Web

We explore the Internet Start page, use a couple of Web search tools, and explore a reference Web site. You also learn how to return quickly to places you have already been, save pages for offline reading, and download files with FTP.

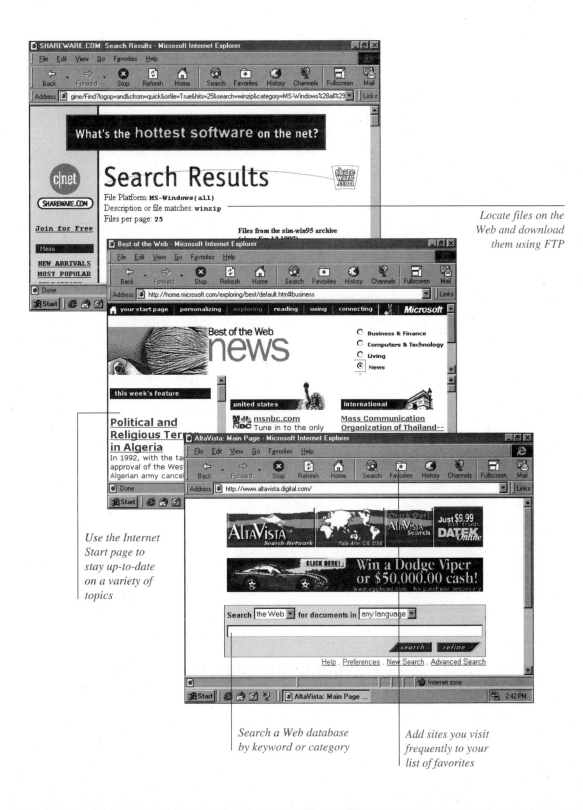

Locate files on the Web and download them using FTP

Use the Internet Start page to stay up-to-date on a variety of topics

Search a Web database by keyword or category

Add sites you visit frequently to your list of favorites

The father of hypertext

The legendary Ted Nelson, a self-taught computer visionary, introduced the concept of hypertext in 1970 in his article "Barnum-Tronics," which was published in the Swarthmore College Alumni Bulletin. The following excerpt from that article was reprinted in his book *Computer Lib/Dream Machines* (1974).

"Hypertexts: new forms of writing, appearing on computer screens, that will branch or perform at the reader's command. A hypertext is a non-sequential piece of writing; only the computer display makes it practical. Somewhere between a book, a TV show and a penny arcade, the hypertext can be a vast tapestry of information, all in plain English (spiced with a few magic tricks on the screen), which the reader may attack and play for the things he wants, branching and jumping on the screen, using simple controls as if he were driving a car. There can be specialized subparts for specialized interests, instant availability of relevancies in all directions, footnotes that are books themselves. Hypertexts will be so much better than ordinary writing that the printed word will wither away. *Real writing by people*, make no mistake, not data banks, robot summaries or other clank. A person is writing to other people, just as before, but on magical paper he can cut up and tie in knots and fly around on."

Until the early 90s, Internet activity was largely confined to government, academic, and research communities and was conducted in boring text formats. Commercial activity was not tolerated (see the tip on page 163). Although large areas of the Internet still operate this way, many users find no reason to explore them. Instead they confine their activity to the World Wide Web, which not only presents its information in graphical formats that appeal to those of us reared on television and special effects, but also embraces capitalism by permitting advertising and online commerce. (It's worth noting that these characteristics go hand in hand. With the most elaborate Web sites costing millions of dollars to produce and maintain, it's not surprising that corporations at the forefront of Web creativity expect to be able to make a buck or two to justify their investment.)

In Chapter 1, we took a look at a Web site using Internet Explorer, and we learned some jargon. Whether you realize it or not, you already know enough to go *surfing*, meaning that you can jump among hyperlinked Web pages, checking out subjects that intrigue you and following topics from site to site across the world. But as appealing as it might be to spend hours exploring cyberspace, if you're like most people, you don't have time for open-ended wandering. Instead, you want to be able to tap into the Internet to find the answers to specific questions. Perhaps you need to track down an IRS form you need to complete your tax return. Or you've been asked to research a piece of equipment your company is considering buying. Or you want to check the traffic patterns in your area to find the quickest route to a downtown meeting with a client. By the time you finish this chapter, you'll know how to use the various mechanisms provided by Internet Explorer and the Web to search for and retrieve the information you need.

Exploring the Internet Start Page

Before we start looking for information, we need to understand a bit about the various ways we can get at the information on the Web. With Internet Explorer, we seem to have a bewildering number of ways to access information, with lots of paths leading to the same places. As you know, when we start Internet Explorer, its Internet Start page is displayed in the viewing area. As well as providing hyperlinks to jump start our excursions on the Web, Microsoft uses this page to tell us the latest news about the company and its products. We'll leave you to explore the Microsoft-specific information on your own. Here, we'll focus on the areas of the Internet Start page that enable us to quickly find other types of information. Let's get started:

1. Connect to your ISP and start Internet Explorer. While the Internet Start page is downloading, notice that Internet Explorer displays a document icon and messages such as *Connecting to site* and *Opening page* at the left end of the status bar. To the right, a blue progress bar shows how much of the download process is complete. Meanwhile, a spinning *e*/globe icon to the right of Internet Explorer's menu bar indicates that the program is busy accessing data and transferring it to your computer. When the word *Done* appears in the status bar, you see the Internet Start page in the viewing area, like this:

The document icon

Hyperlink bar

Text hyperlink

Your Internet Start page will look different from ours because its information changes daily. However, the important navigational tools on the page should be the same as ours unless

Microsoft has radically redesigned the page. (This happens from time to time. Don't let it throw you; a little sleuthing should be all you need to get oriented.) Across the top of the page is a bar of hyperlinks that look something like buttons. They represent tasks you are most likely to want to perform on the Web. Most of these tasks also have fancy text hyperlinks elsewhere on the page.

2. Click the fancy *exploring* hyperlink to display a Start Exploring page something like this one:

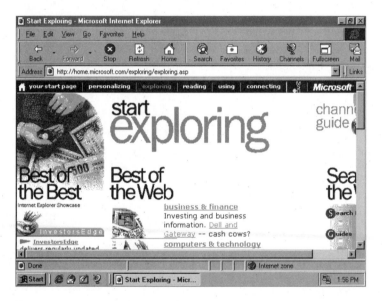

Again, the hyperlink bar appears across the top of the page.

What exactly is a hyperlink?

A hyperlink is a screen element containing embedded coding that specifies the address of the linked site. If you are interested in seeing the coding, simply choose Source from the View menu and scroll about. Hyperlinks are designated by a starting <A HREF = ...> code (the ellipsis is a placeholder for the linked address) and a closing </A> code. The information enclosed in these codes appears as a hyperlink on your screen.

3. Scroll the page noticing all its hyperlinks. (The hyperlinks on this page change frequently, so you might want to check the Start Exploring page often.)

4. Click the Home button on the Internet Explorer toolbar to return to the Internet Start page.

5. Click *exploring* on the hyperlink bar at the top of the page. You move back to the Start Exploring page.

As you have seen, we can access several categories of information from the Start Exploring page. Depending on the type of information we need, we might use this page as a starting point for a search, or as a way of staying up-to-date with the latest news on a variety of topics.

6. Scroll the page and click *news* to jump to this page:

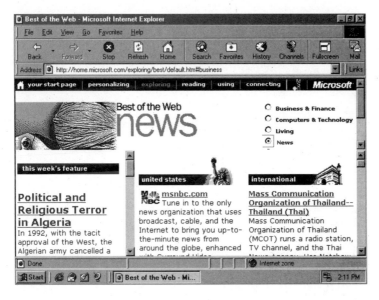

The latest news

This page is divided into frames, each containing separate blocks of information. If the information is too long to fit its frame, a scroll bar appears down the right side of the frame, allowing you to scroll out-of-sight information into view. Again you see the hyperlink bar across the top, as well as the page header and button links to the other categories of information. Then the news information is divided into three broad groups: This Week's Feature appears in one frame, and United States and International appear in another.

7. Scroll a bottom frame, clicking various hyperlinks. Click the Back button on the toolbar each time to return to the News page so that you can take off in a different direction.

8. When you are ready, click the arrow to the right of the Back button to display a list of the places you have visited, and click Start Exploring to return to that page.

Suppose we want to stay up-to-date on news from the financial markets. Follow the steps on the next page to see how we might use the Exploring page to accomplish this goal.

Java

As you surf the Web, you'll notice some sites include moving objects. These objects are rendered by embedded programs called *Java applets*. Java is a programming language developed by Sun Micro-systems that allows Web site developers to include animation and "moving" elements, such as scrolling words, in their pages. Java applets also enable sites to interact with their "visitors." To learn more about Java check out the site at *http://java.sun.com*.

Financial information

1. Click the *business & finance* hyperlink to display this page:

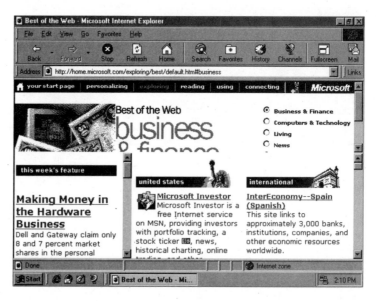

The information sources listed here include financial news, business information services, and portfolio management services, listed in the same three broad groups you saw on the News page.

2. Click various hyperlinks, noting any that provide the type of information you might want to look for later.

3. Click the Back button or use its drop-down list to return to the Start Exploring page.

4. Check out other information categories, until you have an idea of the range of sources represented on the Start Exploring page. In particular, you might want to take a look at the Travel & Entertainment category where you can make reservations. Also browse through the Living category where you can make purchases online. Notice that on all the category pages, the information is grouped under the same three headings, providing a predictable structure for the information.

Travel and entertainment

Online shopping

Having seen how we might browse for current information on a variety of topics, as well as effortlessly spend money, we'll move on to do some more specific research. In the next section, we show you how to gather information about a topic by using various Web search services.

Searching the Web

Suppose we work in the human resources department of a corporation and one of the company's managers has been recently promoted to director of the regional office in Boise, Idaho. The manager has asked us to research the real estate market in Boise to help her relocate and to see if Boise has a gym with a climbing wall. How would we use Internet Explorer and the Web to carry out this task?

To do this kind of research, we need to search a Web database—a collection of information about Web sites and their content. Several databases are available, but we'll look at just a couple of them here. Because the techniques for searching are pretty similar for all the databases, you'll be able to check out the others on your own later.

Web databases are built using a variety of methods. Some rely totally on a program called a *Web crawler* that electronically works its way through the Web gathering information about the sites it finds; others use a Web crawler but also encourage Web-site owners to submit information about their sites for inclusion in the database. (You might hear people talk about *worms*, *spiders*, or *robots*, which are types of crawlers.) Some databases are comprehensive and include everything; others focus on specific types of information. Some do little more than organize the information into categories; others add site reviews and ratings. Because of these construction differences, one database doesn't necessarily contain the same information as another. The two databases we will look at, Yahoo and Alta Vista, are reputed to be among the most comprehensive and to have the most powerful search engines, so searching them should yield some useful information.

Web crawlers

Worms, spiders, and robots

Searching by Category

To demonstrate searching by category, we'll use the Yahoo database, which began its life at Stanford University but has since graduated and become a commercial enterprise. In this example, we'll stick to researching Boise real estate, but you should take the time to check out Yahoo's many features and capabilities on your own. To search for Boise real estate information, follow these steps:

The Search button

1. Assuming you are connected to the Internet and running Internet Explorer, click the Search button on the toolbar. In the Explorer bar that opens, Internet Explorer features one of the available search services:

2. To select a different service, click the arrow to the right of the Select Provider box to drop down a list of those available.

We could begin our search by clicking a service on the provider list, but when we know the URL of the search service we want to use, we've found that it's faster and more efficient to go directly to the service on the Web rather than going through the Internet Start site. Here's how:

1. Click the Search button to close the Explorer bar.

2. Click the URL in the Address box, type *www.yahoo.com*, and press Enter to jump to Yahoo's Web site, which is shown here:

Searching for companies and people

Using Internet resources, you can easily look up names, addresses, e-mail addresses, and phone numbers. See page 86 for more information.

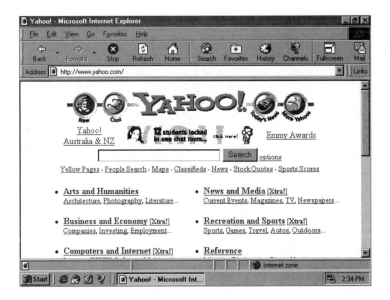

3. Ignore the search box at the top of the page and scroll through the categories, noting their subcategories for future searches.

4. Under *Regional*, click *U.S. States*. Then scroll the page and click *Idaho* in the list of states.

Regional information

5. On the Idaho page, click *Cities*. Then click *Boise* in the list on the Cities page, and click *Real Estate* on the Boise page.

6. Click *Idaho Real Estate*. Internet Explorer jumps from Yahoo to the Web site maintained by the Southwestern Idaho Regional Multiple Listing Service at *www.rmci.net/sirmls/*.

You can now retrieve examples of houses that are currently for sale in Boise by clicking Search.

Searching by Keyword

The alternative to searching a database by category is to search by keyword. We use a *search engine* that matches words we enter in a search box to words in the database. We could use Yahoo's search engine for this example, but instead we'll take another service for a spin. When it comes to searching by keyword, Alta Vista is hard to beat. For this example, we'll enter the words *Boise* and *climbing gym* as keywords. Turn the page and try it.

Security alerts

Throughout this chapter, you will see Security Alert boxes telling you that you are about to send information to the Internet Zone. Because the information you are sending is not private or sensitive, you can simply click Yes to close the box. See page 114 for more information about zones and about Internet Explorer's other types of security.

1. We could click the Search button on Internet Explorer's tool-bar and then click the Alta Vista hyperlink to initiate the search, but as with Yahoo, we'll go directly to Alta Vista's Web site, instead. Type *www.altavista.digital.com* in the Address box and press Enter. Internet Explorer displays this Web site:

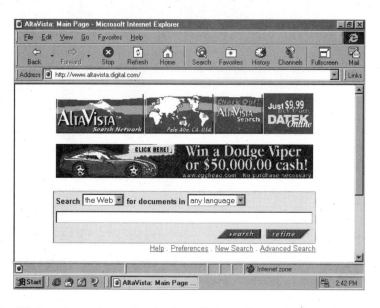

2. Click an insertion point in the edit box above the Search and Refine buttons, type *Boise climbing gym*, and click the Search button. Then scroll the page to see some of the results:

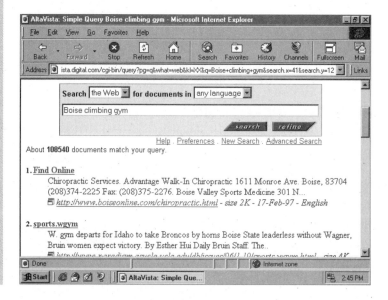

Whoa! What happened here? How could all those Web sites contain the words *Boise* and *climbing gym*? They don't; the sites contain *Boise* or *climbing* or *gym*—or any combination of those words. To get meaningful results from a Web search, we have to construct our search criteria very carefully to narrow down the results as much as possible. For a start, we don't want sites that contain the word *climbing* or the word *gym*; we want sites that contain the phrase *climbing gym*. We'll show you how to make this change with Alta Vista, but bear in mind that different search engines may have slightly different ways of defining search criteria. (Most services have a help feature that gives the specifics for that engine.) Try this:

1. Click an insertion point to the left of the *c* in *climbing* and type " (double quotation mark). Then add another quotation mark after the *m* in *gym* and click Search. The new results are shown here:

Using phrases as search criteria

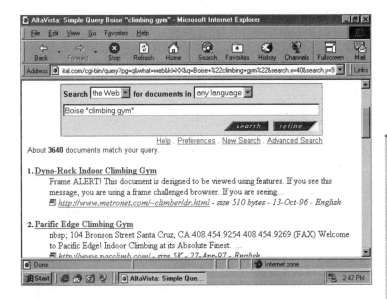

Now we have a list of all the sites containing *Boise* or *climbing gym*. Here's how to narrow the search to those that contain both *Boise* and *climbing gym*:

2. Click an insertion point to the left of the *B* in *Boise* and type + to specify that the matches must contain the following word. Then add a plus sign to the left of the first quotation mark and

Unrelated Web sites

You may be puzzled by the results of some searches, and some found sites may seem irrelevant. If you take the time to examine these sites, which are known as *false drops*, you will probably find one or more of the search terms we entered somewhere in the site's text. If the term is buried, chances are the site isn't what we need, so it's best to focus on those sites whose relevance is obvious. Or the term might have more than one meaning, and your search terms weren't narrow enough to isolate the meaning you want.

click Search. (To exclude a word, type a minus sign.) See what a difference being specific makes:

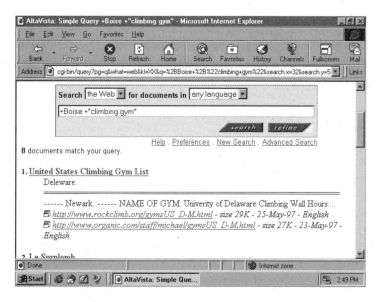

3. Now it is relatively easy to find the information we are looking for. Scroll the page to see the search results. Each of the listed Web sites starts with the site's title (if it has one) and the first few lines of the page. The entry also includes the Web site's URL, the size of the linked file, the date the Web site was added to Alta Vista's database, and the language of the page. (There is a chance that older entries may no longer be valid; either the content may have changed or the site may have moved or disappeared altogether.)

Advanced searches

In Alta Vista, you can click Advanced Search at the top of the page and then enter more complex search criteria. You must use Boolean operators (AND, OR, NOT, or NEAR) between criteria in this type of search. You can also tell Alta Vista to search a specific site element, such as the text or the title. Click the *Help* hyperlink to display a page with more information.

4. Click the *United States Climbing Gym List* hyperlink to display a list of gyms in states beginning with *D* through *M*.

5. Here's a quick way to locate a gym in Boise. Choose Find (On This Page) from the Edit menu to display this dialog box:

6. In the Find What edit box, type *Boise* and click Find Next. Finding text on a page
Internet Explorer searches the text of the displayed page and
displays the first instance of *Boise* that it finds. Click Cancel
to close the dialog box, and scroll the page so that you can
see the information shown here:

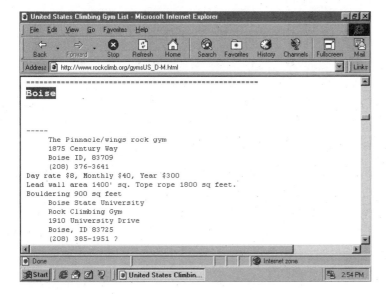

Mission accomplished! All we need to do now is copy the
names and addresses.

Answering Specific Questions

We don't think the Internet will ever replace our dictionary
or phone book, but we can recommend it as a ready source of
answers to several types of simple questions. For example,
suppose we are sending a letter to Princeton, Missouri, and
we don't know the Zip code. We could get on the phone to
the Post Office, but we can also find the answer on the
Internet. The trick is to use a resource like Inter-Links, a Web
site created and maintained by Rob Kabacoff. Try this:

1. With your Internet connection established and Internet Explorer running, type *http://alabanza.com/kabacoff/Inter-Links/*
(the last two words are hyphenated) in the Address box and
press Enter to jump to the Web site shown on the next page.

**If Find doesn't find
anything**

Occasionally, you will use the Find
(On This Page) command to zone
in on a search term in the text of
a site identified in a search and the
term will not be there. So why did
the site show up in the search results? Because you are looking in
the Alta Vista database of Web
sites, not the sites themselves.
Probably the site has changed
since its information was added to
Alta Vista's database.

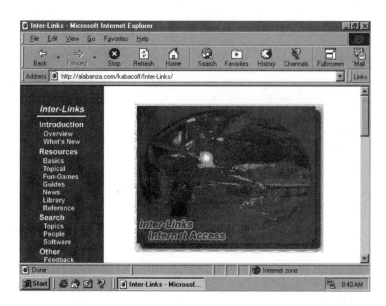

2. Scroll through the Inter-Links home page, which features hyperlinks to lists of more hyperlinks arranged by category. It's well worth exploring this site to get an idea of what kind of information is represented.

Let's start by answering our original question: what is the Zip code for Princeton, Missouri?

1. Click *Reference Shelf*, scroll the list of hyperlinks, and click *Zip Code Lookup*. Internet Explorer accesses a server at the United States Postal Service and displays this Web page:

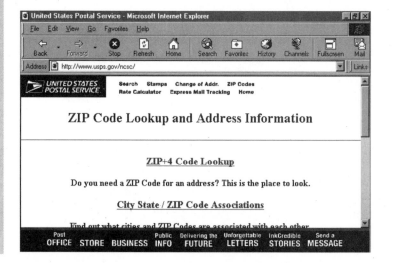

About Inter-Links

The Inter-Links Web site is Rob Kabacoff's "hobby"—meaning that it is not part of his job to maintain the site. As such, this site is typical of the many lists and directories created by Internet "old-timers," who believe that the free exchange of information is what the Internet is all about and who are willing to invest their own time in making information more accessible. You can find out more about Inter-Links and about Rob Kabacoff by clicking the appropriate hyperlinks at the site. If you appreciate all the work he's done, you can even drop him an e-mail message to say "Thanks."

2. Click the *City State / ZIP Code Associations* hyperlink.

3. Next, click the edit box, type *Princeton, MO*, and press Enter or click Process. The page now displays the Zip code.

4. Search for another Zip code, and then click the down arrow to the right of the Back button and select Reference Shelf from the drop-down list to return to the Reference Shelf page.

   Now suppose we want to set up a meeting with a client in a distant city in July 1998 and we are trying to figure out our flight plans so that we can take advantage of cheaper fares by staying over on Saturday night. Bring up an online calendar by following these steps:

1. Scroll the Reference Shelf list and click *Perpetual Calendar*. You see a calendar for the current month.

Checking a date

2. Scroll the page to display the month/year selector, click the arrow to the right of the month, select *Jul* from the drop-down list, enter *1998* as the year, and click Jump. Here's the result:

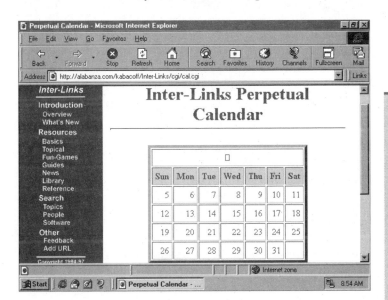

Other useful references

When you are looking for information, you might want to try some of the resources that are listed at the bottom of the Internet Start page. You can also find out how to access a file called *Yanoff's Internet Services List* at *http://spectracom.com/islist/*. Scott Yanoff's list is a compilation of Internet resources often used as a starting point for research projects. (Unfortunately, it isn't updated very often.) And here is another Web site you might try:

http://lcweb.loc.gov
Library of Congress

3. You might want to explore some of the other reference categories before we move on. By pointing to each category, you can see in the status bar whether the linked resource is part of Inter-Links or another Internet resource.

4. When you're done, return to the Inter-Links home page (click the Back button's down arrow and then select *Inter-Links*, or click the arrow to the right of the Address box and select *http://alabanza.com/kabacoff/Inter-Links/*).

Now let's look at some of the other categories of information available from Inter-Links. Suppose we want to contact our US Senators to voice our opinion about a bill that is wending its way through the legislative process. Follow these steps to find out how to reach them:

Finding government
information

1. Click *Topical Resources* on the Inter-Links home page and then click *Government* under *Topics* to display a list of hyperlinks to government resources.

2. Click *Senate Homepage* under *Legislative Branch* to display this Senate Web site, which is located at *www.senate.gov/*:

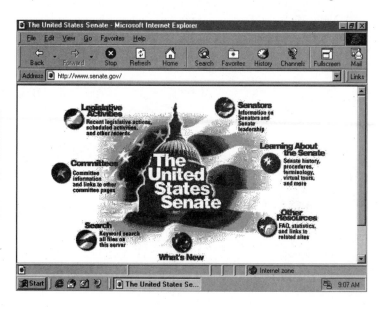

Other government and political sites

Here are some government agencies with Web sites and other political sites you might want to check out:

www.whitehouse.gov
The White House

www.usgs.gov
US Geological Survey

www.nasa.gov
NASA Information Service

www.ed.gov
US Department of Education

www.undp.org
United Nations Development Program

www.odci.gov
The CIA

3. Click the *Senators* hyperlink to display a list of hyperlinks to Senator information.

4. Click *Directory of Senators (by State)*, find your state, and click the name of one of your US Senators to move to his or her home page. For example, here's the home page for Patty Murray, a US Senator from Washington State:

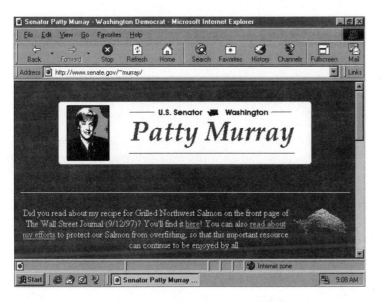

Having found out how to contact our US Senators, we want to check on the progress of the bill in question. Try this:

1. Redisplay the US Government page and click *Thomas: Legislative Information* under *Legislative Branch* to display the Web site maintained by the library of the US Congress at *http://thomas.loc.gov/*:

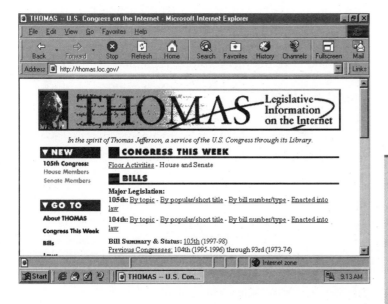

Other ways to retrace your footsteps

To return to the previous page, you can press the Backspace key. To view one of the previous five pages, you can choose the page from the bottom of the File menu. You can also use the History list; see page 98.

2. Scroll through the Thomas home page to get an idea of the information you can access here, and then explore the *Bills* category, following the links of a specific bill.

3. When you've finished, make your way back to the US Government page and check out anything else that interests you. For example, you might want to visit the Web site for the IRS (click *Federal Government - By Agency*, scroll to *Department Of The Treasury*, and click *Internal Revenue Service*, or enter *www.irs.ustreas.gov/prod*). At the time we wrote this book, the IRS published *The Digital Daily*, a sophisticated online newsletter complete with animated graphics and scrolling text instructions. It takes a while to download, but it's often worth the wait.

4. Return to the Inter-Links home page and click your way through any other features that interest you before moving on to the next section.

Returning Quickly to Sites We've Already Visited

We've looked at several Web sites in this chapter, some of which we may want to visit again in another session. It would be a pain to have to write down URLs whenever we find sites we want to return to, and with Internet Explorer, we don't have to. We can add a displayed page to our list of favorite places and have Internet Explorer remember the URL for us.

Using Favorites

Suppose we want to be able to access the Yahoo and Alta Vista home pages without having to always enter their URLs. Follow these steps to add these two search services to our favorites list:

Turning off AutoComplete

If Internet Explorer's attempts to complete your entries in the Address bar bother you, you can turn off the AutoComplete feature. Choose Internet Options from the View menu, click the Advance tab, deselect the Use AutoComplete check box in the Browsing section, and click OK.

1. Type *www.yahoo.com* in the Address box. (Watch the Address bar as you type. You may not have to enter the entire URL because, by default, Internet Explorer remembers URLs you've used before and tries to be helpful by entering them for you using a feature called *AutoComplete*.) Press Enter to display the Yahoo home page.

2. Choose Add To Favorites from the Favorites menu to display this dialog box:

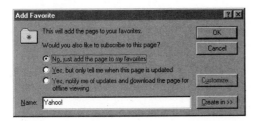

3. You are given the opportunity to subscribe to this page (see the adjacent tip and page 82), but for now just click OK to add the Yahoo page to your favorites list.

4. Now display the Alta Vista page using a different method. Click the History button on the toolbar to open the Explorer bar as shown earlier on page 26. Find *www.altavista.digital.com* (check the lists for other days if it's not on today's list), select Alta Vista Main Page from the sublist, and click the History button to close the Explorer bar.

Using the History list

5. Now right-click a blank area of the Alta Vista home page, choose Add To Favorites from the object menu, and click OK to add the page.

6. Choose Microsoft On The Web and then Microsoft Home Page from the Help menu to display Microsoft's Web site, and then repeat step 5, shortening the entry in the Name edit box to *Microsoft Home Page*.

7. Return quickly to the Yahoo home page by choosing Yahoo! from the bottom of the Favorites menu.

Jumping to a favorite

8. Switch to Alta Vista by choosing Alta Vista Main Page from the Favorites menu.

Organizing Favorites

As we click our way around the Web, we will probably accumulate many favorites, and at some point, too many favorites will detract from our efficiency. Let's add a few more favorites to the list and then organize them into folders for efficient retrieval. Follow the steps on the next page.

Subscribing to Web sites

You can subscribe to a Web site so that you are alerted whenever the site changes to include new information. See page 106 for information about how to subscribe to Web sites.

1. Add favorites for the following URLs by entering each one in the Address box and choosing Add To Favorites from the Favorites menu:

   http://update.wsj.com
   www.nytimes.com
   www.cnn.com

   To read the Wall Street Journal and New York Times Web sites, you need to register to obtain a subscription.

2. Choose Organize Favorites from the Favorites menu to display this window:

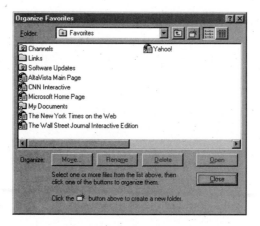

   As you can see, the six favorites you have created are contained in a folder named *Favorites* on your hard drive.

3. Click the Create New Folder button in the dialog box to create a new folder.

4. Type *Daily News* for the folder name and press Enter.

5. Repeat steps 3 and 4 to create a folder called *Search Tools*.

6. Select Alta Vista Main Page and drag it to the Search Tools folder. Then do the same with the Yahoo! favorite.

7. Next, drag the CNN Interactive, The Wall Street Journal Interactive Edition, and The New York Times On The Web favorites to the Daily News folder.

8. Close the Organize Favorites dialog box.

9. Click the Favorites button on the toolbar to display your favorites list in the Explorer bar and see the effects of the new organization. As you can see, clicking Daily News displays a submenu like this one:

The Favorites button

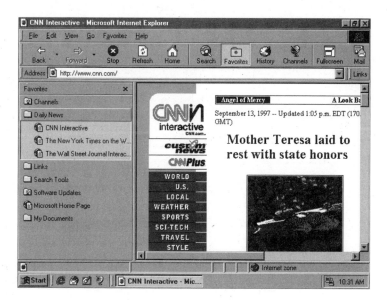

10. Click Favorites again to close the Explorer bar.

Deleting Favorites

Before we leave this discussion of favorites, let's delete the favorite for the Microsoft home page:

1. Choose Organize Favorites from the Favorites menu to open the Organize Favorites dialog box.

2. Select Microsoft Home Page, press the Delete key or click Delete in the dialog box, confirm the deletion, and then close the dialog box.

The deleted favorite is now in the Recycle Bin. If you decide later that you want it after all, you can open the Recycle Bin and retrieve it. Otherwise, it will be deleted completely when the Recycle Bin is emptied.

Predefined favorites

The bottom half of the Favorites menu includes entries for Channels and Links, enabling you to reach the sites on the Channel bar and the Links toolbar by choosing them from the menu. Also included is a Software Updates link that takes you directly to Web sites where you can find new versions of your programs. (Currently, only Microsoft Internet Explorer is listed on the Software Updates submenu.)

Creating Desktop Shortcuts

Suppose we want to be able to view a particular site frequently—for example, to check on a stock's performance. We can create a shortcut to the site on the Windows desktop and then simply double-click the shortcut to both start Internet Explorer and jump immediately to the specified Web site. Here's how:

Stock quotes

1. Type *http://quote.yahoo.com* in the Address box and press Enter to move to the Yahoo! Finance home page, shown here:

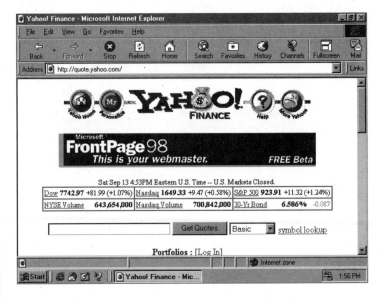

2. For additional practice, create a favorite for the Yahoo Finance Web site.

3. To create the shortcut, right-click a blank area of the page and choose Create Shortcut from the object menu. Internet Explorer displays this dialog box, asking you to confirm the shortcut:

4. Click OK to close the dialog box and confirm the shortcut.

Adding a page to the Links toolbar

Another way to return quickly to a site you visit often is to add a link to that site to the Links toolbar. You can enter the address of the desired page in the Address bar, and then drag the document icon from the left end of the Address bar to the word *Links* on the Links toolbar. Or you can drag a hyperlink directly from a Web page to the word *Links* on the Links toolbar. To delete a page from the Links toolbar, right-click the page's hyperlink and choose Delete from the Object menu.

Now let's test the new shortcut:

1. Close Internet Explorer by clicking its Close button, but don't disconnect from the Internet. On your desktop, you can now see a Yahoo! Finance shortcut icon.

The Yahoo! Finance icon

2. Double-click the Yahoo! Finance shortcut icon. Internet Explorer automatically starts up and takes you directly to the stock quotes page.

3. Click the edit box, type *MSFT* (the code for Microsoft Corporation), and then click Get Quotes. After a few seconds, the current price of Microsoft stock is displayed, along with a variety of performance statistics and news headlines, as shown here:

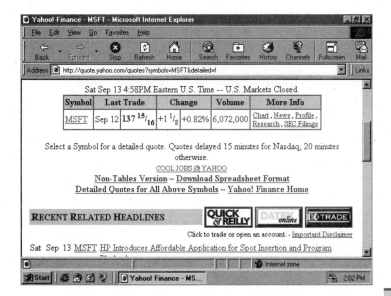

Saving Pages for Offline Reading

Sometimes we will come across a Web page that is full of information we think we need, but ploughing through it all online will take time (and perhaps consume too large a chunk of our Internet access budget). Here, we discuss two ways of avoiding online reading.

Other ways to make Web content available

Desktop shortcuts are a familiar way to provide instant access to programs and information. On page 111, we discuss other ways to put the Web pages you use most frequently on the desktop so that they are never more than a mouse-click away.

The Print button

Printing Pages

The simplest way of saving Web information to read later is to print it. Clicking the Print button on the toolbar prints the current Web page directly to our printer. (If you can't see the Print button, turn off the button labels by choosing Toolbars and then Text Labels from the View menu; see page 96 for more information.) If the printer can handle graphics, they are printed along with the text. The process isn't foolproof. Not all printers handle Web printing well, and some page elements drop out no matter what printer we use. But under ideal conditions, what we get on paper is a pretty accurate rendition of what we see on the screen.

The main advantage of printing pages is that we can read them anywhere. The main disadvantage—apart from using up paper—is that we have to remember where we put the printed pages if we need them later. In the next section, we discuss another technique for offline reading.

Saving Pages

If we want to read a page's information on the computer but offline, we can save the page as a file on our hard disk. (As you'll see in a minute, loading a page from disk can be much faster than accessing it on the Web.) One thing to take into account when saving Web pages is that they can hog a lot of disk space. If all we want is to be able to find the information later, it's more efficient to use favorites and shortcuts. With that in mind, let's create a Web Pages folder and save a couple of Web pages in it. For our first example, we've chosen a page from Microsoft's Web Tutorial. Follow these steps:

1. Choose Web Tutorial from the Help menu and then click the *Internet Basics* hyperlink.

2. Scroll the page and glance at the available hyperlinks. You can always return to them later. Then click *Glossary of Terms* to open the page we want to save for offline reading.

3. Maximize the window and scroll through the page. Reading through all this material would take quite a while, so let's save it as a file that we can read later.

HTML

The World Wide Web is made possible by *Hypertext Markup Language* (HTML). It is enhanced by other coding systems such as Virtual Reality Markup Language (VRML) and by interactive ActiveX and Java components. When you save a file from a Web site, you are given the option of saving it either as an HTML file or as a plain text file. If you select HTML as your Save As Type setting in the Save As dialog box, the file is saved with its HTML coding so that it can be viewed offline in a Web browser. If you select Plain Text, the file is stripped of its coding and can no longer be viewed in a browser. You can, however, open it in a word processing program and view it without formatting there.

4. Choose Save As from the File menu to display the dialog box shown here:

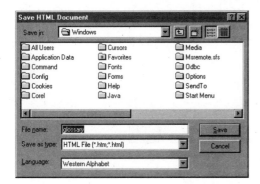

5. With the suggested *glossary* in the File Name box, use the Save In box and the list box to move to the folder where you want to save the page, click the Create New Folder button, name your new folder *Web Pages*, and open it.

6. Leave Save As Type set to HTML File, leave Language set to Western Alphabet, and click the Save button. Internet Explorer saves the displayed page as a file.

Here's how to read the saved page offline:

1. Without quitting Internet Explorer, disconnect from your ISP. You can easily do this by choosing Work Offline from the File menu. (If your Internet configuration does not allow you to do this, end this session completely and then click the Internet Explorer icon on your desktop to restart Internet Explorer, clicking Work Offline if you are asked to reconnect to your ISP.)

← Working offline

2. Choose Open from Internet Explorer's File menu to display the dialog box shown here:

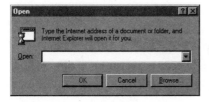

Saving linked pages
Suppose you are viewing a Web site with a hyperlink to a page you want to read offline. You can save the page without displaying it by right-clicking the link and choosing Save Target As from the object menu. (Choose Save Picture As for graphic links.) Name the file and then display and read it as usual.

3. Click Browse to display this dialog box:

4. Move to the Web Pages folder where the Glossary file is stored and double-click the filename to return to the Open dialog box with the name entered in the edit box. Then click OK. In a flash, Internet Explorer loads the page from disk.

5. If you want, you can now read this document in its entirety, without having to worry about running up connect charges.

6. When you have finished reading, close Internet Explorer.

Downloading Files with FTP

So far, we've explored only the part of the Internet known as the World Wide Web, but the Internet includes several other resources that have been around for a long time and are still actively used by Internet veterans who are less concerned with the hype and glitz of the Web than with easy access to information and tools stored on physically remote computers. One of these resources is the *File Transfer Protocol* (or *FTP*), which is used for files that need to be transferred rather than viewed. FTP used to be somewhat clunky and operated in the old-fashioned, text-only manner, but browsers like Internet Explorer make using this resource intuitive and easy.

The File Transfer Protocol

Many computer systems all over the world store files that are available for downloading by any Internet user. Each remote system is set up to display a list of its downloadable files and to allow us to copy a selected file to our computer. The whole process can be accomplished by means of an FTP program built into Internet Explorer. (When we download a file, we copy it from a remote computer—one that is not physically accessible—to our computer. We can reverse the operation and upload a file by copying it from our computer to a remote computer, but because the FTP program included with Internet Explorer does not have uploading capabilities, we don't cover uploading here.)

Why would we want to download a file? Often new users first start exploring FTP when they discover that a new version, bug fix, or enhancement is available for one of their programs. For example, Microsoft frequently announces the availability of downloadable upgrades for its products through its Web site. In the case of these programs, Internet Explorer takes us by means of hyperlinks to the file we need, and we may not realize we are using FTP to download the file. Many shareware and demonstration programs, as well as graphics and text files, are available from FTP servers, but usually the only way of getting at such things is by the deliberate use of FTP.

CAUTION: When you download a file, you should always store it in a temporary folder and scan the folder for viruses before you do anything with the file. You can't "catch" a virus by just looking at a file, but activating a file infected with a virus can wreak havoc. Although viruses usually do their damage via program files, new breeds of viruses attack word-processor and spreadsheet files. So get in the habit of scanning *all* downloaded files with a virus program. Your chances of catching a virus are not great, but recovering from a virus is time-consuming and stressful. It is definitely worth taking a couple of minutes of your time to give all downloaded files a quick check.

Downloading via the Web

In your travels around the Web, you may have come across sites that announced the availability of files for downloading. Often, the name of the file is simply dressed up as a hyperlink, and clicking the link initiates the transfer process. For those of you who have erred on the side of caution and

Can you use it?

Two categories of text and graphics files and three categories of programs are available for downloading on the Internet. Text and graphics files can be:

- In the public domain, meaning that you can freely use them any way you want.

- Copyrighted, meaning that you can use them only if you have the copyright owner's permission and you state that the work is copyrighted and by whom. (There are some "fair use" exceptions.)

Programs can be:

- In the public domain.

- Freeware, meaning that you can freely use the program but, because the program's developer retains copyright to the software, you can't sell it.

- Shareware, meaning that you can use the program for a limited trial period. If you continue to use it, you should register and pay for it. Shareware is an honor system that has produced some great, low-cost programs, and we urge you to keep the programs coming by supporting their developers.

not yet taken advantage of one of these offers, here are the steps for downloading a file from a Web site:

1. With your Internet connection active and Internet Explorer open on your screen, click the *e*/globe icon to the right of the menu bar to go directly to the home page of Microsoft's Web site, which looks like this:

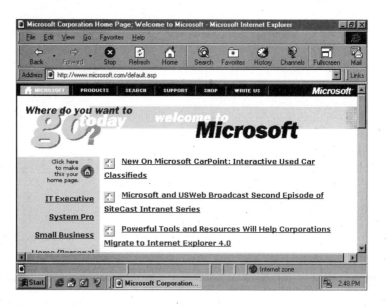

2. You will probably want to explore this Web site on your own later, but for now, simply click the *Support* hyperlink at the top of the page.

3. Scroll the Support page and click *Help Files, Service Packs, & More*.

4. Leave the I Would Like To See All Files option selected, scroll the page if necessary, and click Next.

5. Click the arrow at the right end of the Microsoft Technical Support box, scroll to the bottom of the pop-up list of products, select *Word For Windows Or Macintosh*, and then click *List Files*.

6. Scroll the page to display a list of available files connected with various versions of Microsoft Word:

Compressed files

The last letters of a compressed file's name often tell you what program you need to decompress the file, as follows:

arc, arj	WinZip
hqx (Mac)	BinHex
gz	WinZip
lha	WinZip
sit (Mac)	Stuffit
tar	WinZip
z	WinZip
zip	WinZip

By the way, *gif* and *jpeg* graphics files are compressed files, but you don't need to decompress them to use them because they are automatically decompressed every time you display them.

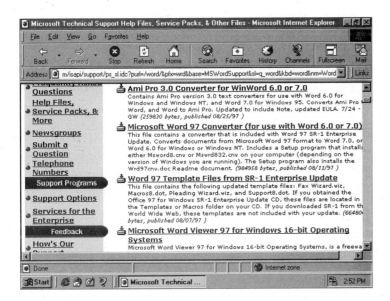

7. Scroll through the list of files and click one you are interested in. (For this demonstration, pick a small file, as indicated by the number of bytes at the end of the description.) What happens next depends on what type of file you click:

• If you click a text or graphic file, Internet Explorer displays it on the screen rather than copying it to your hard disk. To download the file, choose the Save As command from the File menu to display the Save As dialog box.

• If you click a program file, Internet Explorer displays this File Download dialog box, asking whether you want to run the program after downloading it, or save it and run it later:

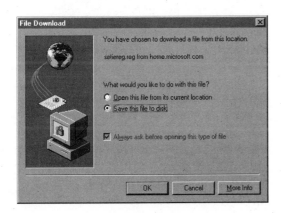

Select the Save This Program To Disk option and click OK. The Save As dialog box appears so that you can select a location for the file.

Creating a folder for downloading files

8. If you have not already created a folder in which to store downloaded files, click the Create New Folder button, type *Download* as the name of the folder, and press Enter.

9. Open the Download folder and click the Save button to store a copy of the selected file in that folder. Internet Explorer then displays a File Download dialog box, reporting its progress and estimating how long the downloading process will take. This estimate is a function of both the speed of your modem and the volume of traffic on the FTP server. If you can't wait the estimated time, you can click Cancel and simply try again later when the server is not quite so busy. The File Download dialog box automatically closes when Internet Explorer has finished downloading the file, and you see a Download Complete message.

10. Click OK to close the message box.

We can now quit Internet Explorer and disconnect from the Internet. After closing the Internet connection, we can run a virus scanner on the contents of the Download folder. However, for this demonstration, let's first move on to see how to access an FTP server directly.

Downloading from an FTP Server

If you kept an eye on the Address box while you were working through the previous example, you may have noticed that only the path part of the URL changed as you made your way through various pages of the Microsoft Web site. Internet Explorer's FTP program worked entirely behind the scenes. In this section, however, we'll give FTP a more active role. Follow these steps:

1. Click the Address box, type *ftp://ftp.microsoft.com*, and press Enter to display the contents of Microsoft's FTP server:

Anonymous FTP

Many FTP servers allow the general public to access specific directories by logging on with the user name *anonymous* and a password that consists of their full e-mail address. (To use other directories, we need an authorized user name and password.) Internet Explorer's FTP program takes care of this login process for us. If you come across a reference that says *use anonymous FTP to download the file*, don't panic. With Internet Explorer, you don't have to do anything unusual to use anonymous FTP.

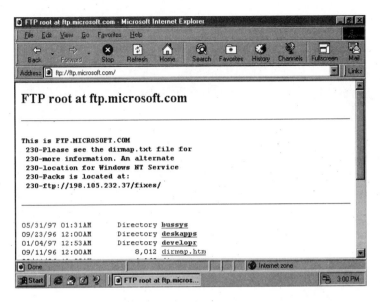

As you can see, Internet Explorer displays directories and files with the dates and times of their last modification and the size of the files.

2. Scroll the window's contents until you see a file called ls-lR.txt, and click the file to display it, like this:

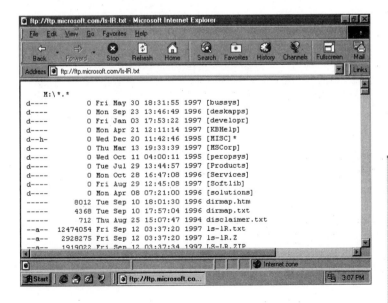

Adding favorites for FTP servers

We can create favorites for all kinds of Internet resources, not just Web sites. For example, to add a favorite for Microsoft's FTP server, simply choose Add to Favorites from the Favorites menu while the top-level list is displayed on the screen.

A *d* in the first column designates a directory (folder) and a − (dash) designates a file. The last entry on each line tells you the directory's or file's name. As cryptic as this list may appear at first, you will probably find it a very useful guide to all the files stored on this FTP server. You will often find lists like this one to help you make your way around the FTP servers you visit.

3. Scroll the list to see how it is structured, and then click the Back button on the toolbar to return to the top-level list of the server's contents.

A compressed version of the file ls-lR.txt is available as LS-LR.ZIP, so instead of downloading the uncompressed list, let's download the compressed file to save time. (Later, we'll download a program to enable us to decompress this file.) Follow these steps:

1. Right-click LS-LR.ZIP and choose Save Target As from the object menu to display the Save As dialog box.

2. Click Save to save the file in the Download folder.

While we are looking at Microsoft's FTP server, we'll show you a very useful source of information about Microsoft products. Follow these steps:

Accessing the Microsoft
KnowledgeBase

1. Click *deskapps* to display the contents of that directory, scroll the list, and click *office*. Then click *kb*. You now see a set of folders containing articles that make up the Microsoft Office KnowledgeBase. (There are *kb* directories for other products, too.) The KnowledgeBase is a repository of information about tips, tricks, and workarounds, as well as a source for updates and bug fixes.

2. Click *index.txt* and then press Ctrl+End to scroll the list to display articles about Office 97, as shown at the top of the facing page.

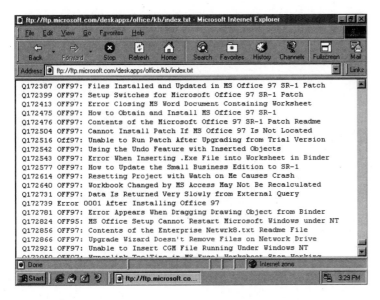

Like ls-lR.txt, index.txt is a standard way of locating specific information on an FTP server. If you want, you can download this list to your Download folder by choosing Save As from the File menu.

3. Find an article you are interested in and note the number on the left. For example, we selected *Q172475 OFF97: How to Obtain and Install MS Office 97 SR-1*.

4. Click the Back button and then use the number to navigate through the folders to the article you have selected. For example, we clicked *Q172*, then *4*, and finally *75.txt*.

5. If you want, save a copy of the article in the Download folder by choosing Save As from the File menu.

Searching for the File We Want to Download

When we want information about a Microsoft product, we can pretty much assume that if it exists, we will find it on Microsoft's FTP server or Web site. But what do we do if we don't know where to look? For example, suppose we want to decompress the LS-LR.ZIP file. We know from the ZIP part of the filename that we need the WinZip shareware program to "unzip" the file (see the tip on page 56). To locate and download the program, follow the steps on the next page.

Archie

If we know the name of the file we are looking for but we don't know where it is stored, we can use a search tool called *Archie* (a corruption of *archive*) to locate the file. The Archie program itself resides on several FTP servers around the world. To find it, enter *Archie* as a keyword in a Web search engine such as Yahoo and click one of the hyperlink results. Then enter the name of the file, and Archie will locate it.

1. Enter *www.shareware.com* in the Address box. (Actually, you could just type *shareware*.)

2. In the Quick Search box, type *winzip* and click the search button. Internet Explorer displays this Web page:

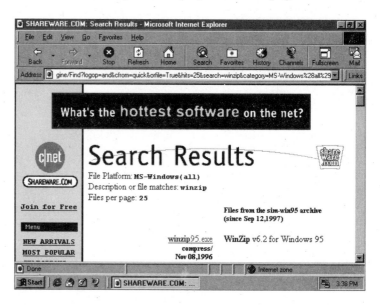

3. Scroll through the list of search results and click the file you want to download. We clicked *winzip95.exe* and scrolled to display the FTP sites in the US, as shown here:

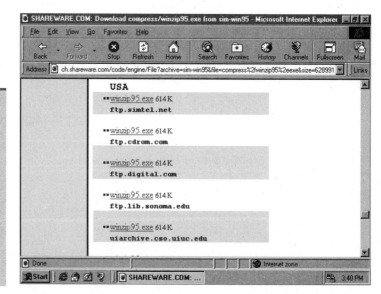

It's all done with mirrors

Popular FTP servers (and popular Web sites) often *mirror* their contents to other computers to provide distributed access to their information. The mirror server stores an exact copy of the parent server. The advantage to the user of this system is faster access; the advantage to the participating servers is reduced duplication of effort.

4. Click one of the USA options. When Internet Explorer displays the File Download dialog box, select Save This Program To Disk, click OK, and then save the program file in the Download folder.

5. If necessary, close Internet Explorer and disconnect from your ISP.

That concludes our demonstration of FTP. Before we do anything with the files we've downloaded, we need to scan the contents of the Download folder for viruses. Next we have to install WinZip by choosing Run from the Start menu, entering the path for the program in the Open edit box, clicking OK, and following the instructions on the screen. And finally, we can use the program to decompress the file that lists the contents of Microsoft's FTP server.

WAIS, telnet, and Gopher

The *Wide Area Information System (or WAIS)* is a set of databases, called *sources*. We can search for information by selecting a source and entering a search query. Instead of searching an index, the WAIS software searches the text of the documents in the source and returns a list of results ranked according to how closely they match the query.

Running *telnet* enables our computer to act as a terminal connected to a computer that stores a program we want to use. We can then run the program on the other computer and see the results on our screen. We can access only the computers that have been set up as telnet servers for use by the public. Internet Explorer doesn't include a telnet program, but Windows 95 does. When we click a telnet link, Internet Explorer runs the telnet program so that we can use the selected telnet server.

Gopher digs up the information stored in non-Web formats on over 6,000 Gopher servers around the world. If you want to take an excursion into Gopherspace, type *gopher://gopher.tc.umn.edu* in the Address box and press Enter to connect to the Gopher server at the University of Minnesota. Internet Explorer displays a "menu" of the server's contents. We can use Veronica (which reportedly means *Very Easy Rodent Oriented Netwide Index to Computerized Archives)* to search an index compiled from the titles of folders and files on all Gopher servers.

Communicating
with Other Internet Users

Using Outlook Express, we show you how to send, reply to, and forward messages. You also learn how to use the Address Book, attach files, organize messages, and find e-mail addresses. We close with a discussion of e-mail conventions and online etiquette.

Compose messages offline
and send them to the Outbox
for later delivery

Receive both company
e-mail and Internet mail
in one Inbox

Use Address Book entries
to simplify the addressing
of messages

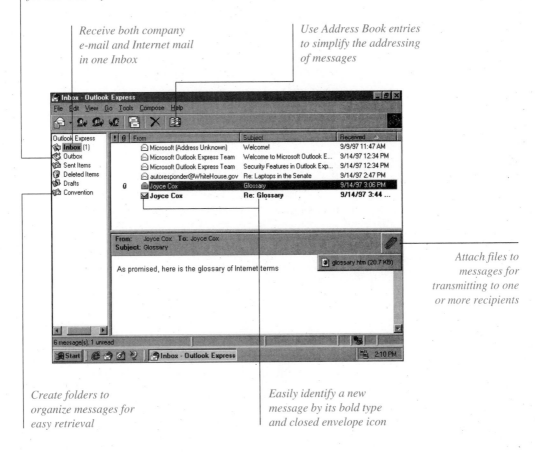

Attach files to
messages for
transmitting to one
or more recipients

Create folders to
organize messages for
easy retrieval

Easily identify a new
message by its bold type
and closed envelope icon

So far, we have focused our attention on the World Wide Web, which is primarily a means of publishing and obtaining information. Although Web sites are becoming more and more interactive, the majority are still passive, one-way channels of communication. In this chapter, we discuss using e-mail for direct, two-way communication with other Internet users. In our examples, we use Outlook Express, the mail program that comes with Internet Explorer 4, but once you have worked your way through this chapter, you will easily be able to transfer your skills to any other mail program you might want to use.

There's nothing difficult about the concept of e-mail. It's simply a way of sending messages that bypasses the traditional post office. The beauty of e-mail is that it doesn't use paper resources, it's fast, and it costs nothing (at least, nothing more than we are already paying for Internet access). Sometimes it is even better than using the phone because it enables us to deal with important business right away rather than run the risk of playing telephone tag. Add to these advantages the ability to include files, programs, and other attachments with the messages we send, and the fact that we can send the same message to several people without any additional effort, and it's easy to understand why even people with abysmal letter-writing habits become staunch advocates of e-mail as a means of communication. Using e-mail, we can fire off a note to someone living on the other side of the world or share our thoughts and ideas with politicians, company presidents, research scientists, and celebrities. (Of course, there's no guarantee that the recipients of our messages will actually read them, let alone respond to them!)

Like any other "good" thing, it's possible to have too much e-mail. Used wisely, e-mail can increase efficiency and reduce the amount of paper we use, but without a little restraint, e-mail can add unnecessarily to the burden of information overload. For example, if we get in the habit of copying messages to our entire department, everyone will feel obliged to spend time reading our messages whether or not they actually need to. Bear in mind this potential for misuse as you begin integrating Internet e-mail into your daily routine.

Inappropriate uses of e-mail

Just as there are inappropriate, and even illegal, uses of traditional mail services, there are also inappropriate uses of e-mail. Harassing or fraudulent e-mail is just as illegal as harassing or fraudulent regular mail. Mass e-mailing (junk e-mail, also called *spam*) and chain e-mailing are definitely frowned on by the Internet community. With regular junk mail, the receiver can decide at a glance whether to spend time and energy opening it. But with junk e-mail, the receiver is forced to spend time and resources (connect charges and hard drive space) before he or she can make that decision. Because of this intrusion, junk e-mails are sometimes punished vigilante-style. The messages have been globally erased using programs called *cancelbots*, and the hard drives of their senders have been swamped by replies that have huge-but-useless file attachments.

Internet E-Mail Concepts

Sometimes people confuse company e-mail with Internet e-mail, and it's easy to understand why because in many ways, they are similar. However, having company e-mail doesn't necessarily mean you have Internet e-mail. To be able to send e-mail to a colleague down the hall via company e-mail, both your computer and your colleague's computer need to be connected to the company's network. To be able to send e-mail to a customer in another state via the Internet, both your computer and your customer's computer need to be able to access the Internet.

Let's briefly look at an example. Suppose we want to use Outlook Express to drop a note to a customer thanking her for a recent order. We open Outlook Express's New Message window, enter the customer's e-mail address in the To box, enter a topic in the Subject box, type the message, and click the Send button on the toolbar. Outlook Express then adds information such as our e-mail address and sends the message from our computer to our ISP's *mail server*, which in turn sends it to the computer designated as the customer's mail server. That mail server holds the message in the customer's *mailbox* until she connects to the server, at which time her e-mail program downloads the message to her hard drive. She can then read and reply to it at her convenience. The reply makes the same journey in reverse: from the customer's computer, it travels first to her mail server and then to our mail server, which holds the reply in our mailbox until we connect to the server, at which time Outlook Express downloads the reply to our hard drive.

← How e-mail works

Obviously, for such a seemingly simple process to succeed as well as it does, some pretty complex things have to happen behind the scenes. A lot of the work rests on the shoulders of two e-mail protocols called *Simple Mail Transfer Protocol* (*SMTP*) and *Post Office Protocol 3* (*POP3*), which control the way messages travel between our computer and our ISP's mail server and between that server and other servers on the Internet. But for the most part, none of that really concerns

← E-mail protocols

us. Once e-mail is set up on our computer, our main responsibility is getting people's Internet e-mail addresses correct.

E-Mail Addresses

E-mail addresses are like postal addresses, but instead of providing five or six items of information to send a letter to someone, we need to provide only a couple of items to send an e-mail. A typical e-mail address looks like this:

jdoe@halcyon.com

If you had to say this e-mail address out loud, you'd say *jay doe at halcyon dot com.*

The user name →

The domain name →

The part of the address to the left of the @ sign is a *user name* that identifies the addressee, and the part to the right of the @ sign is a *domain name* that identifies the mail server where the addressee's mailbox is located. In our example, *jdoe* is the user name and *halcyon.com* is the domain name. (Like URLs, the last part of the domain name—in this case, *.com*—identifies the type of domain; see page 23.)

In the universe of e-mail, many users can have the name *jdoe* and many users can have mailboxes at *halcyon.com*. But only one user named *jdoe* can have a mailbox at *halcyon.com*. In other words, *jdoe@halcyon.com* must be a unique address. If a user named Joe Doe wants a mailbox at *halcyon.com* and *jdoe* already exists, he cannot choose *jdoe* as his user name. Either he must choose a name like *joedoe* so that his e-mail address is *joedoe@halcyon.com*, or he must move his mailbox to a different mail server so that his e-mail address is something like *jdoe@seanet.com*.

Finding people's addresses

You can use the Address Book in Outlook Express to access several popular directory services. In the Address Book, click the Find button, select a directory service from the Look In drop-down box, enter the requested information, and then click Find Now. (Or in Windows, click the Start button, point to Find, and then click People.) For more information about searching for addresses, see page 86.

Obviously, to send e-mail to someone, we must know the correct e-mail address. (See the adjacent tip and page 86 for information about how to track down e-mail addresses.) If we send a note inviting Joe Doe to lunch but address it to *jdoe-@halcyon.com* instead of *joedoe@halcyon.com*, who knows who might show up! More importantly, we might send critical, time-sensitive information off into cyberspace and never know why we didn't get a reply. However, if an e-mail is sent to a nonexistent address, it usually "bounces back," the equivalent of a return-to-sender stamp from the postal service. The moral: double-check the address of the person you want to correspond with before you send a message on its way.

Setting Up E-Mail

If you work for a large organization or you access the Internet through a school computer, e-mail has probably already been set up on your computer. If that is the case, you can skip this section and jump to page 71, where we tell you how to start Outlook Express. If e-mail is not yet set up on your computer, you can't send or receive e-mail until you tell Outlook Express where you want it to store your mail, your name, your user name, the domain names of the servers that will handle your outgoing and incoming messages, and how you access the Internet. As you'll see if you follow these steps, setting up Outlook Express is easy:

1. Obtain the domain names of your outgoing e-mail server and incoming e-mail server from your ISP.

Setting mail options

2. Without connecting to the Internet, start Internet Explorer and specify that you want to work offline.

3. Choose Mail from the Go menu to display this dialog box, in which Outlook Express asks you to select a folder for storing your mail:

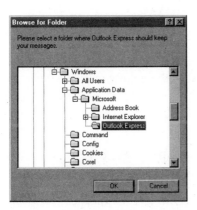

4. Check to make sure the folder selected by default is where you want to store your mail, and click OK. Internet Explorer

then displays the first dialog box of the Internet Connection Wizard, which will guide you through the process of entering your mail settings into Outlook Express:

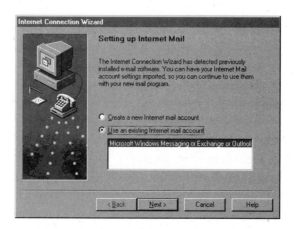

5. Enter the requested information, clicking the Next button to move from one dialog box to the next. If you are unsure about any of the information, click the Help button to get assistance. If you have never used e-mail on your computer before, you will need to enter the following:

- Your first and last name (for example, *Jill Doe*).

- Your full Internet e-mail address (for example, *jdoe@halcyon.com*).

- An Incoming Mail (POP3 or IMAP) Server name and an Outgoing Mail (SMTP) Server name (for example, *mail.halcyon.com* for both).

- A POP account name (probably the name you use when you connect to your ISP; for example, *jdoe*).

- Your password.

- A friendly name that Outlook Express will use for your mail settings (for example, *Jill Doe's Mail*).

- Your Internet connection type. (If you use a modem to connect to your ISP, select Connect Using My Phone Line; otherwise, select Connect Using My Local Area Network.)

6. In the wizard's last dialog box, click Finish to both save your mail settings and start Outlook Express. If you have previously used a different e-mail program on your computer, you see this dialog box:

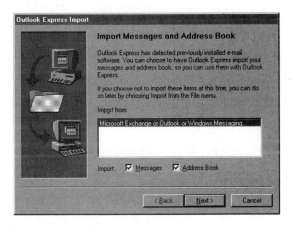

7. Click Next to import your existing messages and address book into Outlook Express, choose a profile name, click OK, and then click Finish. You then see the Outlook Express window.

8. Close Outlook Express, and then close Internet Explorer.

Starting Outlook Express

As you have seen, you can start Outlook Express by opening Internet Explorer and choosing Mail from the Go menu. But you can also go directly to Outlook Express. Try this:

The Outlook Express icon

1. Double-click the Outlook Express icon on the desktop or click the Launch Outlook Express icon on the Quick Launch toolbar. You may see this dialog box:

2. Click Yes or No, depending on your preference. You then see the dialog box shown on the next page.

Working offline

3. Click OK to work offline. You see the Outlook Express window:

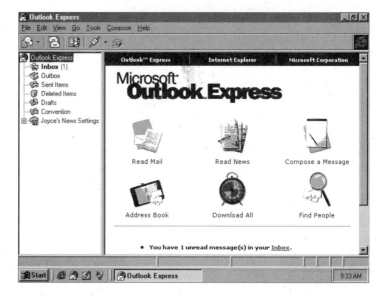

4. Click Read Mail to display this Inbox folder:

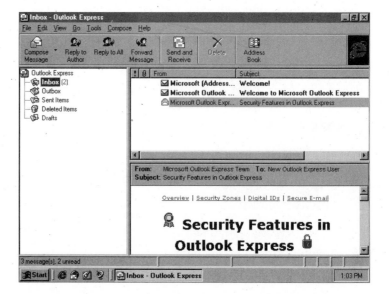

In the left pane is the folder list, used to select a mail folder, such as the Inbox or the Outbox. The selected folder's contents are displayed in the top right pane, and the message selected in that pane is previewed in the bottom right pane.

5. Next, choose Layout from the View menu to display this dialog box:

Turning off button labels

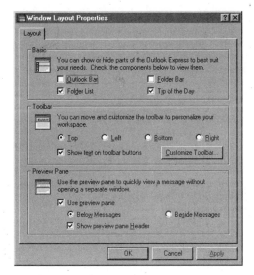

E-mail security

Your e-mail is vulnerable to snooping, as unencrypted e-mail offers as much privacy as a postcard. It is also vulnerable to *spoofing*, as any lout can send e-mail in your name or tamper with an existing message. To prevent both problems, get a *digital ID*, composed of a *public key*, a *private key*, and a *digital signature*. Your public key is used by others to encrypt messages to you, which you decode with your private key. This two-key process is very safe and is possible through irreversible mathematical algorithms. (To encrypt a message, you need the recipient's public key, which you can get from their digitally signed mail. Compatible encryption software is also crucial.) The digital signature affirms that you are the sender and that the message has not been altered en route. Digital IDs are issued by independent agencies, who verify your identity and re-verify the issued ID at certain intervals. VeriSign, Inc. (*www.verisign.com*) offers Microsoft Internet Explorer 4 users a free personal digital ID. Once you have a digital ID, associate it with your e-mail account by choosing Accounts from Outlook Express's Tools menu. Select the desired account, click Properties, and on the Security tab, select Use A Digital ID When Sending Secure Messages, and click Digital ID. Select the ID to assign to this account, and click OK. (To back up your digital ID, choose Internet Options from Internet Explorer's View menu. On the Content tab, click Personal, and click the Export button.) Then to send secure e-mail, click the Encrypt Message button or the Digitally Sign Message button in the New Message window. To automatically encrypt and/or digitally sign messages, choose Options from the Tools menu in Outlook Express. On the Security tab, check the appropriate boxes in the Secure Mail section.

6. Notice the options available in the dialog box, and then click Show Text in the Toolbar section to deselect it, and click OK.

7. Now adjust the width of the left pane by pointing to its right border, holding down the left mouse button, and dragging the double-arrow pointer to the left. You can also adjust the width of columns in the top pane by dragging the borders between column headers.

With that orientation out of the way, let's send a message.

Sending Messages

For this example, imagine we want to remind ourselves to check on a hotel reservation first thing in the morning. As we demonstrate here, we can write messages without being connected to the Internet and then send them when we make the connection. This technique allows us to ensure our messages say what we want them to say, without running up connect-time charges. (Even if you don't have to worry about charges, it makes sense to work offline so that we are not tying up phone lines and taking up bandwidth on a network or an ISP's system.) Follow these steps to compose a message offline:

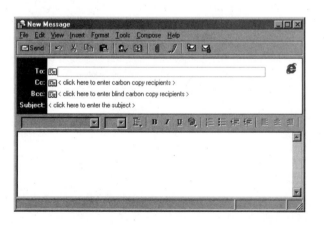

The Compose Message button

1. Click the Compose Message button on the toolbar to display this New Message window:

Message templates

You can click the arrow to the right of the Compose Message button to drop down a list of templates that you can use as the basis for special messages. Simply select a template to display the New Message window with decorated "stationery" designed to complement special-occasion messages, such as party invitations or birthday greetings.

2. In the To box, type your e-mail address and then press Tab to move to the Cc box. (To send a message to someone else, you type his or her e-mail address. To send the same message to

more than one person, you type their addresses one after the other, separated by a comma or a semicolon and a space.)

3. To send a courtesy copy of the message, you can enter the address of the recipient in the Cc box. For this message, leave the Cc box blank by pressing Tab. ◄──────── Sending courtesy copies

4. To send a blind courtesy copy of the message, you can enter the address of the recipient in the Bcc box. For this message, leave the Bcc box blank by pressing Tab.

5. In the Subject box, enter *Seattle reservations* and press Tab. Notice this subject is short and to the point (see the tip below). ◄──────── Specifying the subject

6. Next, type the following in the message area:

Ted said to try the Camlin (1-800-555-0100). It's a renovated hotel within easy walking distance of the convention center.

Your screen now looks like this one:

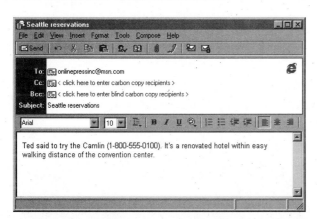

Keep the message's recipient in mind

Some people receive so many messages that they need to be able to distinguish at a glance which they should read immediately and which they can read later. A Subject line like *A New Idea* tells them nothing about the content; *New slogan for Glacier Series* is much better. If the message is time-sensitive, say so by starting the Subject line with the word *Urgent*. If the message does not require any action on the part of the recipient, say so by starting the line with *FYI* (for your information). As for the message itself, avoid long paragraphs, which are hard to read on the screen. Also avoid long messages, limiting them, if possible, to one screenful of information so that the recipient can see the entire message at once.

Urgent messages

By default, all messages are assigned normal priority. If you want to designate a message as urgent, choose Set Priority and then High from the Tools menu of the New Message window. The header of a message with high priority appears in the Inbox preceded by an exclamation mark.

If you want, you can use the buttons on the Formatting toolbar above the message area to format the message.

The Send button

7. Send the message to the Outbox by clicking the Send button. (If you are connected to your ISP, clicking Send instantly sends the message to your ISP's mail server.)

8. If Outlook Express prompts you to connect to your ISP, click Work Offline. If the program displays a message telling you that you can send the message later by choosing Send And Receive from the Tools menu, click the Don't Show option and then click OK to close both the message box and the New Message window. Now the folder list in the left pane indicates that you have one message in your Outbox.

9. Click the Outbox folder to verify that the message is there.

Shortcuts for Addressing Messages

After a while, we'll probably find ourselves e-mailing a few people frequently. We can store their addresses in the Address Book so that we don't have to type them every time. Follow these steps to add an address to the Address Book:

The Address Book button

1. Click the Address Book button on the toolbar to display the window shown at the top of the facing page.

Signatures

To create a signature that will appear at the bottom of your messages, such as your name, title, company, and phone number, choose Stationery from the Tools menu, click the Signature button in the bottom section, and type the text of the signature in the edit box. (Keep it short and avoid being cute.) Click the Add check box if you want to add the signature to all messages and click OK. You can add the signature to specific messages by clicking the Insert Signature button on the New Message window's toolbar.

Business cards

To create an electronic business card, enter yourself in the Address Book and then select your name from the Address Book list. Then choose Export from the File menu, and click Business Card. You can add this card to all of your messages the same way you would add a signature (see left), or you can add your card to individual messages by simply choosing the Business Card command from the Insert menu.

Using groups

If you frequently send messages to a set of people, you can create a group in the Address Book. Click the New Group button on the Address Book's toolbar, assign the group a name, and click OK. Then either click New Contact to create a listing for someone new or click Select Members to add an existing address, and click OK. Enter the name of the group in the To box of the New Message window and press Tab to enter the e-mail addresses of everyone in the group.

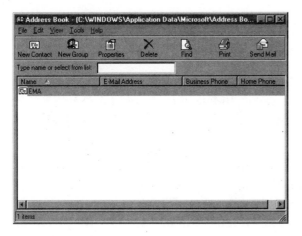

2. Next, click the New Contact button on the toolbar to see this dialog box:

The New Contact button

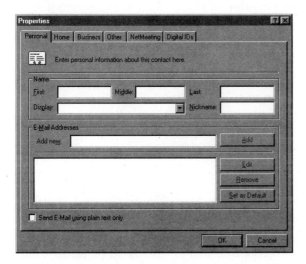

3. In the Name section, type *Mr.* for the first name and *President* for the last name. Type *pres* (or any short, memorable word that strikes your fancy) in the Nickname box. In the Add New box of the E-Mail Addresses section, type *president@whitehouse.gov* and then click the Add button next to it.

4. Click OK to add this contact to the Address Book.

5. Then click the New Contact button on the toolbar and repeat steps 3 and 4 to add your own e-mail address to the Address Book with the nickname *me*.

Other Address Book options

You can organize your Address Book in a number of ways. To sort the information by first or last name, e-mail address, or phone number, simply click the respective column header. Clicking the header again will reverse the sort order (ascending vs. descending). To view only mailing groups, choose Groups List from the View menu and select the group to display its members. If you want to erase a contact or group, select the entry and click the Delete button. If you want to convert a group member to an individual entry, double-click the group name, select the contact name from the Members list, and click Remove. You can print the Address Book information by selecting the relevant entries, clicking the Print button, and choosing a print style: Memo (all data), Business Card, or Phone List.

Now let's try sending another message, this time using the Address Book to see how it speeds up the addressing process. Follow these steps:

1. With the Address Book window open, right-click *Mr. President* and choose Send Mail from the object menu. Outlook Express opens the New Message window with the correct e-mail address already in the To box.

2. Fill in the Subject box, type a message to the President, and then click the Send button to send the message to the Outbox. (After the message is sent, you will probably receive an automated acknowledgment from the White House, or you might even be chosen to get a response from a member of the President's staff.)

3. Finally, close the Address Book window and notice that the Outbox folder now contains two messages waiting for transmission.

Attaching Files to Messages

With Outlook Express, we can send files with our messages. For example, suppose we want to send the glossary file we downloaded in Chapter 2 to a colleague. The following steps, which use your own e-mail address instead of a colleague's, demonstrate the process:

1. In the Outlook Express window, click the Compose Message button to open the New Message window, type *me* (the nickname for your e-mail address) in the To box, and press Tab. Outlook Express will send the message to the corresponding address in the Address Book.

2. Press Tab twice to skip over the Cc and Bcc boxes.

3. In the Subject box, type *Glossary* and press Tab.

4. In the message area, type *As promised, here is the glossary of Internet terms* and press Enter.

Attaching a picture

You can easily attach a picture to a message. Make sure that Rich Text (HTML) is chosen on the New Message window's Format menu and that Send Picture With Message is chosen on the Tools menu. (If they are not, choose Options from the Outlook Express Tools menu, and on the Send tab, click HTML in the Mail Sending Format section, click the Settings button, click the Send Pictures With Messages option, and click OK.) In the message area of the New Message window, click an insertion point where you want the image to appear, and then choose Picture from the Insert menu. Click Browse to find the desired image file, double-click its filename, and click OK in the Picture dialog box to insert the file. Send the message as usual.

5. Click the Insert File button on the toolbar to display this dialog box, in which you can select the file you want to attach to the message:

The Insert File button

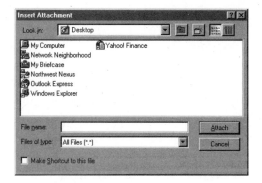

6. Move to the Web Pages folder where the glossary file is stored and double-click its filename. In the New Message window, *glossary.htm* now appears as an icon in a new frame below the message, as shown here:

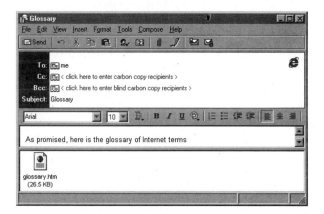

7. Click the Send button to store the message in the Outbox.

Sending Messages Stored in the Outbox

We now have three messages stored in Outlook Express's Outbox folder, waiting for us to connect to the Internet so that they can be sent on their way. Here's how to send the messages:

1. Click the Outbox folder in the left pane of the Outlook Express window to see the messages.

Attaching a Web page

If you want to send a hyperlink to a Web page with a message, first make sure Rich Text (HTML) is chosen on the New Message window's Format menu. In the body of the message, you can simply type a Web site's URL to create an active link to that site. Or you can select the text that will serve as the link, click the Insert Hyperlink button on the Formatting toolbar, select the resource type, enter the path to the linked site, and click OK. Then simply send the message the way you usually do.

The Send And Receive
button

2. Click the Send And Receive button on the toolbar. Outlook Express displays this dialog box:

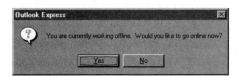

3. Click Yes. Outlook Express initiates the connection to your ISP, sends the messages, and checks for any new incoming messages. (You may be asked to enter your mailbox password during the process.)

Retrieving and Handling Messages

We can retrieve any messages that are waiting in our mailbox on our mail server by clicking the Send And Receive button on the toolbar. (As you've seen, clicking the Send And Receive button also sends any messages waiting in the Outbox.) Usually, we will want to keep Outlook Express open while we work on the Internet so that we can receive any new messages. Outlook Express will check the mail server for new messages according to the schedule we set on the General tab of the Options dialog box (see the adjacent tip).

When we have Outlook Express set up to retrieve messages according to a schedule, the program notifies us when we receive a new message, displays an envelope icon at the right end of the taskbar, and plays a sound to alert us to the new arrival. Here's how to manually retrieve messages:

New message alert

1. Click the Inbox folder in the window's left pane to display the message headers in the top right pane.

Scheduling mail delivery

If you are connected to your ISP and running Outlook Express, by default the program checks the server every minute for new messages. You can change this schedule by choosing Options from the Outlook Express Tools menu, and adjusting the Check For New Messages setting.

2. If you don't see at least two new messages in your Inbox, click the Send And Receive button on the toolbar. (In addition to messages from the Microsoft Outlook Express Team and the two messages we sent to ourselves, you might see a response from the White House.)

3. Drag the borders of the columns in the top pane to adjust their widths like this:

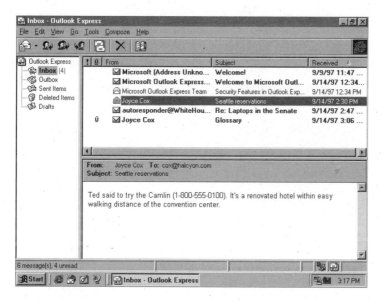

Let's take a closer look at the Inbox. In the top right pane is the sender's name, the subject, and the date and time we received the message. When we have not yet displayed a message, an unopened envelope is shown next to the sender's name, and the message header is displayed in bold type. An exclamation mark in the first column indicates that the message is urgent, and a paperclip in the second column indicates that the message has an attachment.

Here's how to read a message:

1. In the top pane, click the Glossary message. Mail displays the message in the preview pane below and after a few seconds changes the unopened envelope to an opened one, like this:

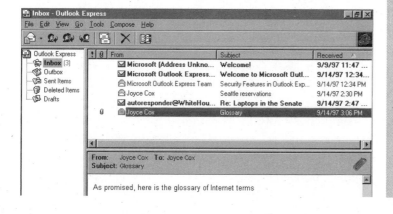

More about reading messages

You can scroll the preview pane to read a selected message, and you can reply to it by clicking the buttons on the Outlook Express toolbar. By default, if you display a message in the preview pane for 5 seconds, Outlook Express presumes you have read it and opens its envelope icon and changes its type. (You can change this setting by choosing Options from the Tools menu, clicking the Read tab and adjusting the Message Is Read option.) If a message is long, you can display it in its own window by double-clicking the message header in the top right pane. You can mark a read message as unread or vice versa by right-clicking its header and choosing Mark As Unread or Mark As Read from the object menu.

2. Click the paperclip in the header of the bottom pane, which tells you the message has an attachment, and then click the attached filename. Outlook Express displays this dialog box:

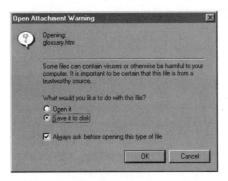

3. Click OK to save the attached file, naming it *glossary2*.

Replying to Messages

Suppose this message is from a colleague and requires a response. Follow these steps to send a reply:

The Reply To Author button

1. With the Glossary message displayed in the preview pane, click the Reply To Author button on the toolbar to open a window like this one:

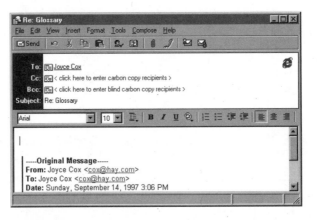

The Reply To All button

Notice that the To and Subject boxes are already filled in. (Clicking the Reply To All button displays a similar window, except that the To box contains not only the address of the original sender but also those of all recipients of carbon copies.) Notice also that the original message appears at the bottom of the message area preceded by a vertical line. Outlook Express has inserted this text because the Include Message In Reply option is selected by default on the Send tab of the dialog box displayed when you choose Options from the Outlook Express Tools menu.

2. Type *Thanks. Great stuff!* and click the Send button. Outlook Express sends the reply on its way if you are still connected to the Internet, or puts it in the Outbox if you are working offline.

3. So that you can see how the reply looks, click the Send And Receive button and check out the new message when it arrives.

Forwarding Messages

If we receive a message that we think will be of interest to a colleague, we can forward the message with a few mouse clicks. Here's how:

1. Click the *Seattle reservations* message and then click the Forward Message button on the toolbar to display this window:

The Forward Message button

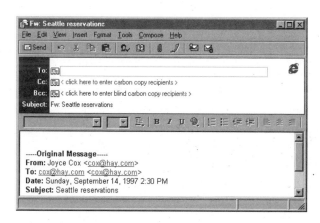

2. For demonstration purposes, type *me* in the To box.

3. Click an insertion point in the message area, type *Here's where we're all staying*, press Enter, and click the Send button on the toolbar.

Moving among unread messages

When you have several messages in your Inbox, it is easy to catch up with the unread mail. Simply choose Next and then Next Unread Message from the View menu. You can also press Ctrl+U to jump from one unread message to another.

4. So that you can see how a forwarded message looks, click the Send And Receive button to retrieve the new message.

Deleting Messages

In the early days of e-mail, people would often hang onto old e-mail messages so that they had a record of their senders' addresses. Because it is easy to add e-mail addresses to the Address Book, that particular reason for keeping old messages no longer exists. After we have finished reading many of our messages, we will probably want to delete them. To demonstrate how to delete messages, we'll clean up the Sent Items folder, but bear in mind that the procedure is the same for any folder. Follow these steps:

1. Click the Sent Items folder in the left pane to display the headers of all the messages you have sent. (Outlook Express stores copies of your sent messages in this folder because the Save Copy Of Sent Messages option is selected by default on the Send tab of the Options dialog box.)

The Delete button

2. Choose Select All from the Edit menu and click the Delete button on the toolbar.

3. Click the Deleted Items folder in the left pane and notice that the deleted files have simply been transferred there, giving you an opportunity to change your mind about deleting them.

Emptying the Deleted Items folder

4. You really do want to delete these files, so right-click the Deleted Items folder, choose Empty Folder from the object menu, and click Yes to confirm that you want to discard them.

Organizing Messages

When we first started Outlook Express, the program provided five folders: Inbox, Outbox, Sent Items, Deleted Items, and Drafts. In addition to these program-generated folders, we can create folders of our own to help organize messages in logical ways. (Some people prefer to create folders in which to store all their messages so that the Inbox acts as a temporary receptacle for new messages only.) Let's create a folder and move some messages into it now:

1. Right-click Outlook Express in the left pane and choose New Folder from the object menu to display this dialog box:

Creating folders

2. Type *Convention* in the Folder Name edit box and press Enter.

3. Click the Inbox folder, select the *Seattle reservations* message, and drag it to the Convention folder.

Moving messages

4. Here's another way to move messages. Right-click the *FW: Seattle reservations* message, choose Move To from the object menu, select the Convention folder in the Move dialog box, and click OK.

5. Click the Convention folder in the left pane to display the messages in their new location, like this:

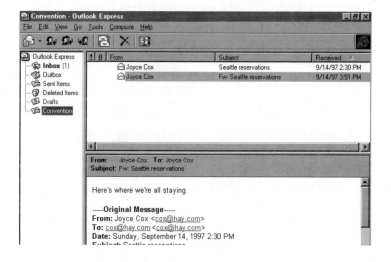

Finding People's E-Mail Addresses

Once you have e-mail, you'll probably use it whenever you can for both business and personal communications. The one big stumbling block will be obtaining the necessary e-mail addresses. Suppose we've been asked to research the feasibility of exporting our company's products to the Far East, and we remember hearing that a former colleague recently toured several Far Eastern countries with a US trade delegation. We want to touch base with her to see if she can point us to some information sources. Or suppose we have been thinking lately how different our lives would have been if one of our teachers hadn't coaxed us into taking Advanced Placement Biology rather than sticking with easy courses. We want to let him know how we're doing and to thank him for taking an interest when he did. How can we send e-mail messages to these people if we don't know their e-mail addresses?

One way to track down the e-mail addresses of individuals and companies is through Internet "white pages" directories. Access to several of these directories is built into Outlook Express. In this section, we'll show you how to use a directory called *Four11* (pronounced *four one one* for the old telephone directory inquiries service). Follow these steps:

Four11

1. With the Outlook Express Inbox open, choose Find People from the Edit menu to display this Find People dialog box:

In the main Outlook Express window, you can click the Find People icon to display this dialog box.

2. Click the arrow at the right end of the Look In box and select Four11 from the drop-down list.

3. Type a name in the Name box and click Find Now. For example, here is the result when you enter *Ken Griffey*:

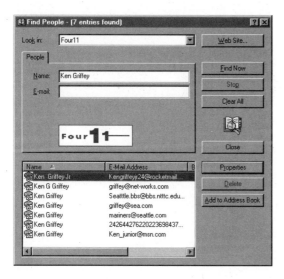

This type of search is not infallible. Although Four11 claims to have over 10 million listings, there's a chance you'll pick a name that is not in its directory or that yields many listings, none of which seems to be the person you are looking for. (For more information, click the Web Site button in the Find People dialog box to display the Four11 home page.)

4. You can select an address and click Add To Address Book to save the address for later use. But for now, click Close to close the Find People dialog box.

5. Close Outlook Express and disconnect from your ISP.

Style and Etiquette

We'll wind up this discussion by passing along a few e-mail conventions. (Your company may have its own set of *do's* and *don'ts*, especially for communications with customers.)

People are often much more casual about the tone and language they use in e-mail messages than in letters. By and

Tone and language

large, a less formal approach is appropriate, unless we are communicating with customers or the company CEO. However, *less formal* doesn't mean *sloppy*; we should still check spelling and proofread for grammatical mistakes before sending our messages on their way. And *less formal* doesn't mean *unthinking*; we should still be careful about how we express ourselves. Many people think of e-mail as an electronic form of conversation. But without facial expressions, body language, and voice inflections, words in an e-mail message can easily be misunderstood. To mitigate this problem, the online community has adopted the following techniques for adding emphasis and indicating humor, amazement, or anger:

Emphasis

• **Capital letters.** Generally, capital letters should be used sparingly in messages because they add varying degrees of emphasis. Using initial capital letters draws attention to words Without Stressing Them. Writing an entire word in capital letters DOES stress the word. An entire phrase or sentence in capital letters is very emphatic and SHOULD BE AVOIDED unless appropriate for the context of the message.

WRITING AN ENTIRE PARAGRAPH OR MESSAGE IN CAPITAL LETTERS NOT ONLY MAKES THE PARAGRAPH HARD TO READ BUT IS ALSO THE E-MAIL EQUIVALENT OF SHOUTING AND MAY BE INTERPRETED AS RUDE. EVEN IF YOU HAVE A LEGITIMATE GRIPE, THINK TWICE BEFORE FIRING OFF A MESSAGE IN ALL CAPS.

Flaming

Sending rude messages, called *flaming*, is generally frowned on and can provoke irrational responses.

Emphasis and profanity

• **Punctuation.** The asterisk can be used to add *mild* emphasis to a specific word. The exclamation mark in conjunction with capital letters can ensure that a !!!VERY IMPORTANT POINT!!! gets made. Strings of question marks and exclamation marks denote confusion, but strings of other punctuation marks are commonly interpreted as placeholders for swear words, as in *??!!??Why did you call him a #$%&@*??!!??*

- **Emoticons.** Also called *smileys*, emoticons are combinations of characters which, when viewed sideways, resemble facial expressions. You either love them and sprinkle them liberally all over your e-mail messages, or you hate them and find other ways to indicate how you feel about what you are writing. Here is a list of some common emoticons and their meanings:

  ◄─────────────

  Expressions

:-)	*I'm happy*
:-(	*I'm not happy*
:-c	*I'm very unhappy*
;-)	*I'm kidding (wink)*
:-D	*I'm laughing*
:-o	*I'm amazed*
<:-<	*I'm angry*
:-@	*I'm screaming*
%-)	*I'm confused*

  These guidelines apply not only to e-mail but to other forms of online communication, such as newsgroups, which we discuss in Chapter 6.

TWO

PART

BUILDING PROFICIENCY

In Part Two, we build on the techniques you learned in Part One to round out your Internet Explorer skills. After completing these chapters, you will know enough to put Internet Explorer to work, streamlining your Web access and facilitating communication both within your company and with the outside world. In Chapter 4, you customize Internet Explorer to increase your efficiency. In Chapter 5, you explore other ways of communicating, including using NetMeeting and your own Web pages. In Chapter 6, you take a look at newsgroups, a valuable source of collective wisdom about a wide variety of topics.

4

Customizing
Internet Explorer

We customize the program window and adjust display speed. Then we change the starting page and show you how to access the Web directly from the desktop. And finally, we fine-tune Internet Explorer's security features.

*Turn off the toolbars and
use commands on menus
to get around*

*Move the Address bar
into the menu bar to
gain viewing space*

*Use active Web content
and channels to access
Web information from the
desktop*

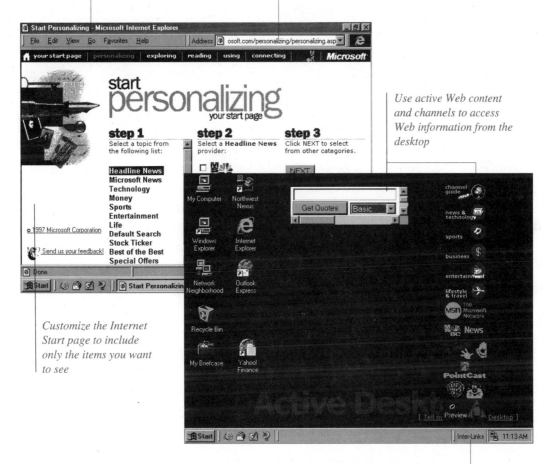

*Customize the Internet
Start page to include
only the items you want
to see*

*Add Web-site toolbars to
the taskbar for instant
access at any time*

Internet Explorer's default settings control the way the program looks on the screen and, to a certain extent, the way Web sites appear in the viewing area. We can change these settings at any time, and in the first part of this chapter, we show you how to customize Internet Explorer to suit the way you work. Then we move on to more sophisticated customization. We personalize the Internet Start page and change Internet Explorer's starting page so that the information we use the most is displayed when the program starts. Then we look at ways to make the information we want to see easily accessible even when we are not running Internet Explorer. Finally, we show you how to fine-tune Internet Explorer's security features to take care of some of the safety issues we discussed in this book's Introduction (see page xiii).

Customizing the Display

We can tailor the display to meet our needs in a variety of ways. Customizing some of the features puts our own decorative stamp on Internet Explorer's interface (its way of presenting information). Customizing others, like the first set of items we'll discuss, can have an impact on our working efficiency.

Enlarging the Viewing Area

In the examples we've covered so far, we've used Internet Explorer's default settings, but these settings eat up viewing space. In this section, we talk about some ways you can give Web pages a little more elbow room on the screen.

Manipulating the Menu Bar and Toolbars

The components of the Internet Explorer program window take up a considerable portion of the screen, especially on a 14- or 15-inch monitor. You can decrease the amount of space consumed by the program window by turning some of these elements off. Follow these steps:

1. Without connecting to your ISP, start Internet Explorer.

The Fullscreen button

2. Click the Fullscreen button on the toolbar. The dramatic result is shown at the top of the facing page.

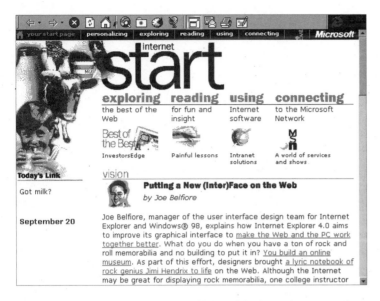

Internet Explorer has turned off the title bar, the menu bar, the status bar, the taskbar, and all but the Standard toolbar, which now appears without labels at the top of the screen.

3. Move the pointer over the buttons on the toolbar. Internet Explorer uses the Windows ToolTips feature to display each button's label as you point to it.

ToolTips

4. Suppose you aren't comfortable letting go of all the navigational aids just yet. Click the Fullscreen button again to toggle it off and to restore the program window to its former state.

If Fullscreen seems a bit drastic, we can manipulate the window components individually. Try this:

1. Choose Toolbars from the View menu to see this submenu:

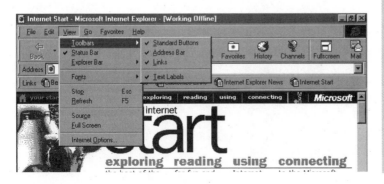

Changing the font size

Another way to get more text on the screen is to shrink the size of the font used to display Web pages. (The font sizes are generally defined by the pages' designers to achieve a desired effect, but usually Internet Explorer can override the designers' specifications.) Choose Fonts from the View menu to display a submenu of relative sizes, and then choose either Smaller or Smallest to shrink the font.

The commands on this menu are *toggles*, meaning that you choose them once to turn them on and choose them again to turn them off. When a toggle is turned on, Internet Explorer puts a check mark beside it.

Turning off button labels

2. Choose Text Labels from the submenu to turn off the labels on the buttons, like this:

Because the buttons now display only icons, they shrink in both height and width. Now they not only give you a little extra viewing room, but on a 14- or 15-inch monitor you can see buttons that were formerly out of view.

3. Point to a button to have Internet Explorer display the button's name. As you can see, you don't really need the labels to know what each button does.

Shrinking the toolbar buttons has helped a bit, but suppose we want even more space for displaying Web pages. Follow these steps:

Turning off window components

1. Right-click anywhere on the toolbar and in turn, choose Links, Address Bar, and Standard Buttons to turn them off. (You can also turn off the status bar by choosing its command from the View menu.) The corresponding Internet Explorer components disappear from the screen, and the top of your screen now looks like this:

Small toolbar buttons

You can shrink the size of the buttons on the Standard toolbar even further. Choose Internet Options from the View menu, click the Advanced tab, scroll to the Toolbar section, select the Small Icons check box, and click OK. Even if you have button labels turned on, the buttons are still smaller than regular buttons.

2. Now how do you get around? Click *Go* on the menu bar to drop-down a menu that includes these commands:

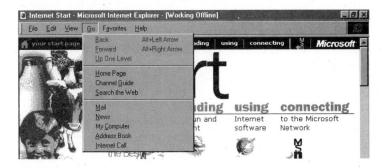

As you can see, some of the buttons from the Links bar are represented here as commands, and this menu also provides command equivalents for the Back, Forward, and Up buttons.

3. Check out the other menus and make a mental note of the locations of commands that replace other buttons you use.

How do you enter a URL to move to a different Web site when the Address bar is turned off? Like this:

1. Choose Open from the File menu to display this dialog box:

Opening URLs

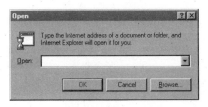

2. Type *www.yahoo.com* in the Open edit box and press Enter to jump to Yahoo's Web site. (This site should be stored on your hard drive and should be available even though you are working offline. If Internet Explorer wants to go online to find the Yahoo site, tell the program not to bother and continue working offline.)

This method of moving to a different Web site introduces a few extra steps, so turn the page to find out about another way of keeping the Address bar at hand without taking up screen "real estate."

Redisplaying window
components

1. Choose Toolbars and then Address Bar from the View menu to redisplay the Address bar.

Moving the Address bar into
the menu bar

2. Point to the word *Address* at the left end of the bar, hold down the left mouse button, and when the pointer changes to a double arrow, drag the Address bar up into the blank area at the right end of the menu bar. Release the mouse button when the Address bar is in the correct position and is about the size of the longest URL you expect to type. Here's the result:

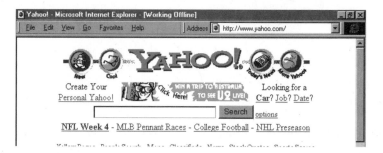

Now suppose you frequently use the Explorer bar to get from place to place. With our new window configuration, the Explorer bar options are just a menu-command away. Try this:

Displaying the Explorer bar
with menu commands

1. Choose Explorer Bar from the View menu to see this submenu:

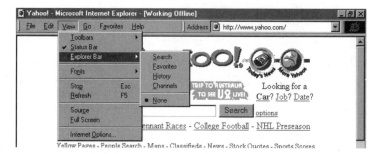

Sizing the Explorer bar

You can make the Explorer bar wider or narrower by dragging its right border to the right or left. You might want to decrease its width to the minimum size and then leave it open while you view Web pages in the main viewing area.

The bullet beside None indicates that nothing is currently displayed in the Explorer bar, so it is closed. Unlike the toolbar options, only one Explorer bar option can be selected at a time.

2. As an example, choose History to open the Explorer bar so that you can access Web pages you've recently visited.

3. Click the Close button (the X) on the History title bar to close the Explorer bar.

Changes we make to the program window remain in effect until we change them again. We can always come back later and reset these options any way we want them.

Turning Off the Taskbar

You probably already know that you can turn off the taskbar at the bottom of the screen to gain some space. Follow these steps to try it now:

1. Right-click a blank area of the taskbar and choose Properties from the object menu. You see this dialog box:

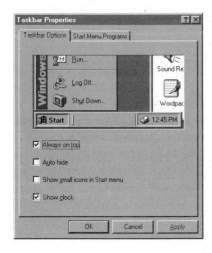

2. Click the Auto Hide option to select it, then click OK, and finally click a blank area of the Internet Explorer window to make sure that window is active. The taskbar disappears, and the Internet Explorer window expands to fill up the newly available space.

3. Point to the bottom of the screen to make the taskbar temporarily reappear, and then move the pointer away from the bottom of the screen to hide the taskbar again.

   Temporarily redisplaying the taskbar

4. Turn the taskbar back on by displaying it, right-clicking it, choosing Properties, deselecting Auto Hide, and clicking OK.

   Permanently redisplaying the taskbar

   In a later section, we'll show you how to take advantage of the taskbar to put Web information at your fingertips even when you are not running Internet Explorer (see page 110).

Speeding Up Page Display

Heavy traffic on the Web can slow us down just like heavy highway traffic can. Animation, video clips, sound, and pictures all give Web pages pizazz, but they can take forever to download. One simple way to speed up page display is to tell Internet Explorer not to bother with these elements. As a demonstration, we'll visit a multimedia site and test its download speed both with and without its multimedia components:

1. Choose Work Offline from the File menu to deselect it, connect to your ISP, and open the CNN Interactive page at *www.cnn.com* by choosing it from the Daily News folder of your favorites list.

No need to wait →

2. Before Internet Explorer has fully downloaded the page, click any hyperlink to move on. Notice that you don't have to wait until everything is in place to get on with your work.

It doesn't take more than a couple of visits to graphic-rich Web sites like CNN Interactive to figure out that, although they are attractive, downloading them can be slow. Suppose all we want to do is get in, glance at the news headlines, and move on. Follow these steps to tell Internet Explorer to block some of the turtle-speed components:

1. Choose Internet Options from the View menu and click the Advanced tab to display these options:

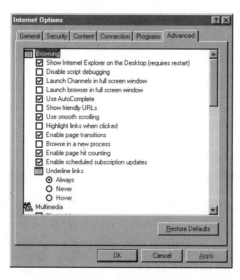

Stopping in mid-access

If we grow impatient while waiting for Internet Explorer to display a Web page, we can always click the Stop button on the toolbar to abort the downloading process.

2. Scroll down to the Multimedia category, deselect the Show Pictures check box, and click OK.

3. Now click the *e*/globe icon at the right end of the menu bar to load Microsoft's home page. Scroll through the page, noticing the graphic placeholder frames, which look like this:

◄— Quickly accessing the Microsoft Web site

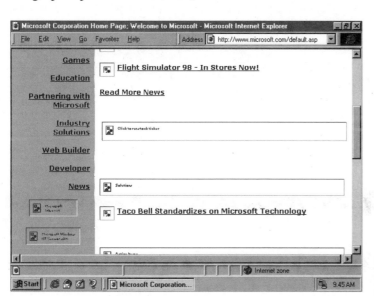

4. Right-click a placeholder, choose Show Picture from the object menu to display only that graphic, and then scroll the page, noticing that other graphics still have placeholders.

5. Return to the Advanced tab of the Internet Options dialog box, select the Show Pictures check box, and click OK.

6. Choose Refresh from the View menu. (When the Standard toolbar is displayed, you can click the Refresh button.) Graphics appear in place of all the placeholders.

Personalizing the Internet Start Page

As we saw in Chapter 2, Internet Explorer provides many avenues for accessing information. However, one of the most efficient ways of quickly reaching the information we need is to personalize the Internet Start page so that it includes links to the Web sites we visit regularly. In this example, our goal is to keep things as simple as possible so that we can get in

Increasing temporary storage space

As you view Web pages, Internet Explorer stores them as files in a folder on your hard drive. The next time you want to see a page you have already viewed, the program can display the page quicker because it can access the folder on your hard drive faster than it can the Web. However, the folder is allowed to grow only to a specified size, at which point, older pages are discarded. You can speed up the display of pages you visit often by increasing the folder's maximum size. Choose Internet Options from the View menu and click the Settings button on the General tab. Drag the Amount Of Disk Space To Use slider to the right and click OK twice.

Creating a custom page via MSN

You can create your own starting page using a feature of The Microsoft Network (MSN). Display the MSN home page by typing *www.msn.com* in the Address box. Click the *Custom* hyperlink and scroll through the notes at the top of the page. Then type your name in the first box, fill in any other boxes you want, and select a color and a background sound. (Click the name of each sound file to hear a sample.) Specify a tabbed page, which uses hyperlinks to jump to linked pages, or a scrolling page, which puts everything on one long page. Specify whether you want to receive promotional e-mails from Microsoft. Under *Favorite Links*, enter up to five hyperlinks to other sites. Next, add your custom page to your favorites list so that you can easily return to it. If you want to further customize your page, scroll down and complete the remaining options. (You can always return to this page and change it later.) To view the results, jump to the bottom of the page by clicking any of the *Here* buttons and then click the View Your Custom Page button. The specifications for your custom page are stored on your computer, and the page is rebuilt from these specifications every time you click the *Custom* hyperlink. You can change the specifications by displaying the custom page, clicking the *Change Custom Options* hyperlink, and making new selections for all the page components.

and out quickly without having to wade through a lot of extraneous information. Follow these steps:

1. Choose Home Page from the Go menu to move to the Internet Start page.

2. Scroll to the Your Personal Choices section, which looks like this:

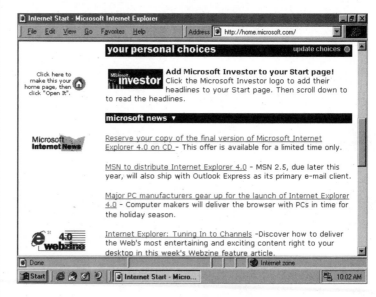

3. Press Ctrl+Home to move to the top of the page, and then click the Personalizing hyperlink to display this page:

4. Headline News is currently selected in the Step 1 column. You don't want to see Headline News, so deselect the option in the Step 2 column and click Next in the Step 3 column to record your preference and move to Microsoft News in the Step 1 column.

Removing categories

5. You don't want to see Microsoft News either, so deselect its Step 2 options and click Next in Step 3.

6. You don't want to see the next five categories in the Step 1 column, so click Next for each to leave their Step 2 settings deselected.

7. For Default Search, select Alta Vista as your search engine in the Step 2 column and click Next.

Adding categories

8. Deselect any Step 2 options for the remaining Step 1 categories.

9. Now suppose you decide you want to add travel information to your Internet Start page. Click Life in the Step 1 column, select Expedia in the Step 2 column, and click Finish in the Step 3 column. You return to the standard Internet Start page, where nothing seems to have changed.

10. Scroll down to the Your Personal Choices section, which now looks like this:

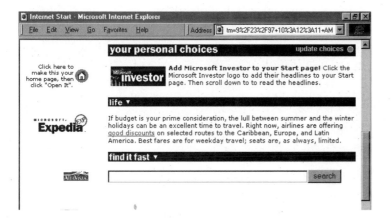

Suppose you change your mind about wanting news from Microsoft that could be useful to your work. Turn the page to learn how to change Your Personal Choices.

Changing Your Personal Choices →

1. Click the Update Choices button at the right end of Your Personal Choices to jump to the Start Personalizing page.

2. Click Microsoft News in the Step 1 column, select both options in the Step 2 column, and click Finish in the Step 3 column.

3. When you return to the Internet Start page, scroll down to see your updated choices.

Switching the Home Page

By default, Internet Explorer's home page is the Internet Start page produced by Microsoft. Although Microsoft takes advantage of our visits to this page to push its products, it also provides enough Web services, plus headline news, to make this default acceptable to a good many Internet Explorer users. But suppose your company has its own Web site and you want to check out the latest corporate announcements each time you log onto the Internet. Or suppose you want to check the calendar of today's events on your school's Web site. Since we can add the Internet Start page to our favorites list to easily access its services at any time, it may make sense to change Internet Explorer's default home page.

As an example of how to change the home page, we'll use the Inter-Links Web site, which provides access to many useful resouces (see page 42). Follow these steps to change Internet Explorer's home page so that Inter-Links is displayed whenever we start the program or whenever we click the Home button on the toolbar:

1. Move to the Inter-Links site by selecting it from the History list (see page 98), selecting it from the Address bar's drop-down menu, or typing *http://alabanza.com/kabacoff/Inter-Links/* in the Address bar.

2. Choose Internet Options from the View menu and in the Home Page section of the General tab, click Use Current and click OK.

Now for the acid test:

1. Close Internet Explorer.

Starting with a blank "page"

If you don't want to check a particular Web site every time you start Internet Explorer, you can start the program with a blank viewing area so that you don't have to wait for the home page to load. In the Internet Options dialog box, specify that you want Internet Explorer to start with a blank page by clicking the Use Blank button in the Home Page section and clicking OK.

2. Start Internet Explorer again. After a few seconds, you see the Inter-Links home page on your screen.

3. Choose Home Page from the Go menu. Internet Explorer reloads the Inter-Links home page.

We can now use the hyperlinks on this page or open another Web site using any of the methods we covered in Chapter 2.

Integrating the Web with the Desktop

The Internet has grown so big so fast that the amount of information available is overwhelming. To solve the problem of information overload, we want to focus on just a few sources that we can rely on to deliver the information we need when we need it, with the least investment of our own time and effort. And we want to customize our computers so that the information comes to us automatically; we don't want to go hunting for it all the time.

A new technology called *Webcasting* has been developed to respond to this need by combining the concepts of TV broadcasting and the Web. Like TV broadcasting, Webcasting organizes information into channels, but it also allows us to pick and choose what we see in a way that goes beyond the simple TV model.

Webcasting

In Internet Explorer 4, Webcasting has been implemented by means of an overhaul of the Windows desktop. In Chapter 1, we discussed some of the desktop changes, but we stopped short of showing you the most exciting aspect of the Windows Desktop Update, which goes by the name of *Active Desktop*. This new feature allows us to customize our computers to provide constant access to specified Web sites while we are using other tools to perform our daily tasks. In this section, we explore a few ways to put the power of the Web at our fingertips even when we are not actively running Internet Explorer. First we'll lay some groundwork by looking at how to subscribe to Web sites so that we are notified when their material is updated.

Active Desktop

Subscribing to Web Sites

When we showed you how to create favorites in Chapter 2 (see page 46), we mentioned that we would cover the subscribing options in the Add Favorite dialog box later. Let's revisit that dialog box and see what subscribing is all about:

Weather information

1. With your connection to your ISP active and Internet Explorer running, type *www.weather.com* in the Address bar and press Enter. Then scroll the page, type your city in the Enter A City edit box, and click the Go City button. Internet Explorer displays a Web page like the one shown here for Seattle:

2. Choose Add To Favorites from the Favorites menu to display the dialog box shown earlier on page 47.

3. Click the Yes, But Only Tell Me When This Page Is Updated option, and then click the Customize button to start the Subscription Wizard.

4. Enter the requested information, click Finish to close the wizard, and then click OK to add the subscribed site to your favorites list.

Now suppose you decide you want the day's weather delivered to your computer every morning. Here's how to change the subscription settings:

1. Choose Manage Subscriptions from the Favorites menu to display this window (we've enlarged it quite a bit):

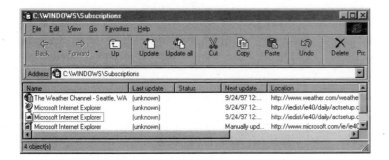

2. Right-click The Weather Channel, choose Properties from the object menu, and then click the Receiving tab to display these options:

3. Click the Notify Me...And Download option, click the Schedule tab, and click the New button to display the Custom Schedule dialog box shown on the next page.

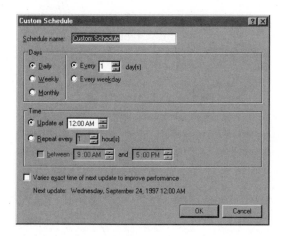

4. Type *Daily at 9* in the Schedule Name box and change the time to the right of Update At to 9:00 AM. Then click OK twice.

5. Finally, close the Subscriptions window.

Now every morning at 9:00, Internet Explorer will download the weather report ready for us to read offline. (Obviously, our computer must be turned on and Internet Explorer must be running for the transfer to take place.) We know when the report has been updated because a red asterisk appears with its icon on our favorites list. Choosing The Weather Channel from the favorites list then displays the updated Web site.

Using Channels

We can take another step into the world of Webcasting by using Internet Explorer's Channel bar. You may already have displayed the Channel bar by clicking the Channel button on the toolbar, but you can also display the Channel bar and work with it directly on the desktop, by following these steps:

The Channel button

1. Close Internet Explorer.

2. Right-click the desktop and choose Active Desktop and then View As Web Page from the object menu. Your desktop now looks something like the one on the top of the facing page.

Deleting channels

To delete buttons from the Channel bar, we right-click the category, choose Delete from the object menu, and then confirm the deletion.

We can click any of the channel buttons to see icons for all the available channels for that category. For example, this is what we saw when we clicked News & Technology:

Clicking an icon displays a preview page for that channel, which includes a button we can click to subscribe to that channel. Clicking the button displays an Add Subscription dialog box like the Add Favorites dialog box shown on page 47. Clicking OK adds the channel to our subscription list and downloads the channel's information to our hard drive. (This can take quite a while.) We can accept the default download schedule or customize it (see page 107). When the transfer is complete, the channel's home page is displayed full-screen and we can use all the usual techniques to move around, gathering the information we need. When we have finished,

PointCast

The PointCast channel provides access to one of the pioneers of Webcasting technology. Billed as an *Internet news network*, Point-Cast is a customizable compilation of headlines from a variety of sources, providing up-to-date news from around the world. The service is advertiser-supported (no fee), so be prepared for the commercials. But if a one-stop news source is what you're looking for, you might want to take the PointCast channel for a test drive.

we click the Close button in the top right corner to return to the desktop, where a button for the subscribed channel has been added to the bottom of the Channel bar.

To get an up-to-date overview of all the channels available, we can click Channel Guide at the top of the bar to move to Microsoft's Active Channel Web site. Here, onscreen directions give instructions for subscribing to channels. We suggest you poke around in this Web site, adding any channels you think might be useful, and then come back and join us for the next section.

Adding Web Content to the Desktop

The concept of adding Web content to the desktop is not hard to grasp, but different people will take advantage of it in different ways. In this section, we'll show you a couple of techniques and leave it to you to decide how to use Web content to make your daily work easier. As an example, suppose we have a Web site we refer to often and we want to keep it close at hand. We can add Web content to the taskbar by following these steps:

Putting items on the taskbar →
1. Right-click the taskbar, choose Toolbars and then New Toolbar from the object menu, type *http://www.alabanza.com/-kabacoff/Inter-Links/* in the edit box, and click OK. Now the taskbar looks like this:

Sizing the taskbar

If you want to add several new Web-site toolbars to the taskbar but can't fit them all in, you can point to the top border of the taskbar and drag upward to create a "double-decker" taskbar. You can then try arranging all your Web-site toolbars on one deck, while retaining the other deck for program buttons.

2. Point to the vertical bar to the left of Inter-Links, hold down the left mouse button, and drag the two-headed arrow to the right until all you can see of the toolbar is its name.

3. To display the Inter-Links home page, right-click its toolbar and choose Open In Window from the object menu. Internet Explorer starts with the page in the viewing area. Click the Close button to close the window.

If our taskbar tends to get crowded, we might want to put the Web link directly on the desktop, instead. Try this:

1. Right-click the desktop, choose Properties from the object menu, and click the Web tab to display these options:

◄ Putting items on the desktop

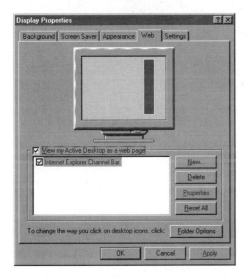

2. Click the New button and when Internet Explorer asks whether you want to select an item from the Active Desktop Gallery (see the adjacent tip), click No.

3. Click the Browse button and double-click Yahoo! Finance in the list of favorites to return to the New Active Desktop Item dialog box with that page's URL in the Location edit box. Click OK to close the dialog box and OK again to add the subscribed item without specifying a password.

4. After Internet Explorer downloads the site information, click OK to close the Properties dialog box.

5. Back on your desktop, use the vertical scroll bar to scroll the Yahoo! Finance page until you can see the edit box where you enter stock codes. Then size the active item by dragging its frame until only the edit box and the Get Quotes button are visible. Finally, point to the top of the item to display a "title bar" and drag the bar to move the item to the top of the screen, where it looks like the one at the top of the next page.

The Active Desktop Gallery

To make it easier to add items to your desktop, Microsoft maintains the Active Desktop Gallery, a collection of Web sites that are likely candidates for active items. You access the gallery by clicking Yes in the New Active Desktop Item message box (displayed in the adjacent step 2). Internet Explorer starts and takes you to the Active Desktop Gallery page at Microsoft's Web site. You can then select any available item to display a preview, and click the Add To My Desktop button at the bottom of the preview page if you like what you see.

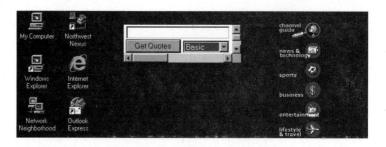

6. Type *MSFT* in the edit box and click the Get Quotes button. Internet Explorer starts and displays the Yahoo! Finance page, which you can scroll to see the latest price of Microsoft stock.

7. Click the Close button to close Internet Explorer.

Active items on your desktop might slow down your computer somewhat, so let's delete these two items for now (you can always experiment later):

1. Right-click the taskbar and choose Toolbars and then Inter-Links to turn off your custom toolbar.

2. Right-click the desktop, choose Properties, click the Web tab, deselect the *http://quote.yahoo.com* check box, and click OK.

You might think that putting items on the desktop would be inconvenient because the desktop is often covered up by whatever application you are working with. But when you have the Quick Launch toolbar displayed on the taskbar, a simple click of the Show Desktop button minimizes all active windows and reveals the desktop. So go ahead and experiment as much as you like with adding active content to your desktop so that it is never more than one click away.

The Show Desktop button

Customizing for Security

In the Introduction to this book, we discussed various aspects of Internet security and mentioned that Internet Explorer provides several mechanisms for protecting ourselves against the relatively small risks we take when using the Internet. In this section, we discuss how to customize Internet Explorer to give us some peace of mind.

Managing Cookies

You'll recall from our discussion in the Introduction (see page xiii) that a cookie is a file sent to our computer's hard drive by a Web site so that the file can store information about us and our activities on that site. When we return to that URL, a program at the Web site checks the cookie file to see what we did the last time we visited. The cookie might be used only to develop site demographics, or it could potentially be used as a basis for tailoring our visits—for example, when we enter the site's URL, the site could automatically load the page where we spend most of our time, instead of the home page.

By default, Internet Explorer allows Web sites to store their cookies on our computer's hard drive. But the whole idea of little programs working stealthily behind the scenes to gather information about our habits and preferences, no matter how innocuous or limited the information, gives some people the heebie-jeebies. If you are one of them, you can tell Internet Explorer not to accept any cookies. Alternatively, you can specify that you want to approve all cookies before they are accepted. As a demonstration, here are the steps for setting up cookie approval:

1. Start Internet Explorer, choose Internet Options from the View menu, click the Advanced tab, and scroll down to the Cookies section, which is nested in the Security section:

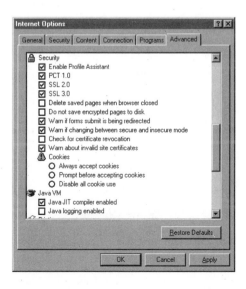

Where are cookies stored?

The cookies files are stored in a subfolder of the Windows folder called (surprise!) *Cookies*. If you're interested, you can use Windows Explorer to find a cookie file with today's date, right-click it, and choose Quick View from the object menu to see what it looks like.

2. Select Prompt Before Accepting Cookies and click OK.

3. To test the change, type *www.wired.com* in the Address bar and press Enter. You see this security alert:

4. Click Yes or No, depending on your preference.

5. After viewing the online version of *Wired* magazine, choose Home Page from the View menu to return to familiar territory.

If we click No, some Web sites will allow us to view their pages but will try resending their cookies periodically. Some sites won't allow us to view their pages at all until we accept their cookies. If we get tired of dealing with the Security Alert dialog box, we can always return to the Advanced tab of the Internet Options dialog box and set the Cookies option to Always Accept Cookies.

Securing the System with Security Zones

Another area of security we may be concerned about is protecting our computer from the malignant diseases that can be introduced purposely or accidentally when we download files or run programs across the Internet. Internet Explorer fights contagion with a system of security zones that enable you to identify the sites you trust to send files to your computer and those you don't. Internet Explorer comes with four predefined security zones to which we can assign specific sites. We can then set the security level for each zone to reflect the extent to which we trust the assigned sites. Follow these steps to see how zones work:

1. Select Internet Options from the View menu and then click the Security tab of the Internet Options dialog box to display these options:

Profile Assistant and Microsoft Wallet

As the Internet becomes more pervasive, we are increasingly asked to divulge personal information in order to tap into its resources. Some Web sites require that we supply information about ourselves before we can view them. Others require that we transmit address and payment information in order to make online purchases. To simplify the process of supplying this information, we can use the Profile Assistant to store and encrypt personal details and Microsoft Wallet to transmit credit card information without fear of it being purloined in transit. Web sites designed to work with both Profile Assistant and Microsoft Wallet can then request the information in its secure form from these programs, and we can approve or deny the request. (We will still have to deal manually with sites that are not set up to work with these "helpers.") To set up these programs, choose Internet Options from the View menu, click the Content tab, and then use the Edit Profile, Addresses, and Payments buttons in the Personal Information section to enter the required information, which is then encrypted to keep it secure on our own hard drive as well as out in cyberspace.

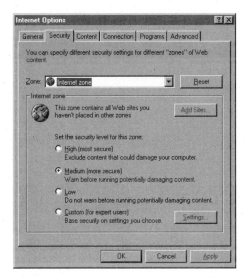

The default security level for the Internet Zone is Medium, meaning that you will be warned about any potentially damaging files that will be downloaded from sites in this zone (including the Java applets that make pictures and text on a Web page move). Notice that the Add Sites button is not available for this zone, because all sites not assigned to the other three zones are automatically members of the Internet Zone.

2. Click the arrow to the right of the Zone box and select Trusted Sites Zone from the drop-down list. The default security level for the Trusted Sites Zone is Low, meaning that you will not be warned about files downloaded from sites in this zone.

3. Click the Add Sites button to display this dialog box:

Internet Zone

Certificates

Certificates are used primarily by secure sites that want to be able to conduct their business over the Internet. They are issued by independent organizations, and they are date-stamped so that Internet Explorer can check not only that the certificate is valid but also that it is current before downloading information from that site. If a site does not have a certificate, if the certificate has a different address from the site, or if the certificate has expired, Internet Explorer notifies us of the discrepancy, and we can decide whether to risk proceeding or whether to do business only with trusted sites whose certificates Internet Explorer is able to authenticate.

Be careful about which sites you add to the Trusted Sites Zone, because you can never be totally sure about the files you are downloading. Also bear in mind that your company may have rules about which sites can be assigned to this zone.

4. Deselect the Require Server Verification check box, type *http://www.microsoft.com* in the Add This Web Site edit box, click Add, and then click OK.

Restricted Sites Zone → 5. Click the arrow to the right of the Zone box and select Restricted Sites Zone from the drop-down list. The default security level for the Restricted Sites Zone is High, meaning that files that could potentially damage your computer will not be downloaded from sites in this zone.

6. Click OK to close the dialog box without adding any sites to the Restricted Sites Zone.

When we are viewing a Web page, the site's zone is displayed at the right end of the Internet Explorer's status bar, so we know at a glance whether we trust that site and whether we should initiate any file transfers.

Censoring Web-Site Content

If you work in a big city, you know that if you take a certain route to get to work, you'll have to turn a blind eye to some of the unsavory characters and establishments you'll see along the way. Even if you are prepared to handle the experience in the interests of getting from point A to point B as quickly as possible, you wouldn't want your kid sister or brother wandering around in that neighborhood. The Internet is like a huge city, with all its diversity, both up-scale and down. If we want to tilt that scale so that we never see the **Content Advisor** → lower end, we can turn to Content Advisor, which blocks access to sites that contain offensive material. Follow these steps to set up Content Advisor:

1. Choose Internet Options from the View menu, click the Content tab of the Internet Options dialog box, and click Enable in the Content Advisor section. Internet Explorer displays a dialog box so that you can create a supervisor password.

2. Type a password, confirm it, and click OK. You then see this dialog box:

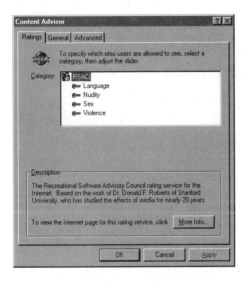

3. Set the level for each category by selecting it and moving its rating slider. If you don't want any offensive language, nudity, sex, or violence, leave the sliders for all the categories set at Level 0 (all the way to the left).

4. When you are finished setting the content levels, click OK.

Now when anyone attempts to use your computer to display a Web site that is rated higher than the levels you set for language, nudity, sex, or violence, Internet Explorer blocks it. However, it's important to note that this technology is relatively new, that a great many Web sites don't yet have content ratings, and that the system is not totally foolproof. Obviously, sites with material that many people would deem offensive aren't going to seek a rating if the rating's only function is to provide a mechanism for blocking the site. By default, Content Advisor blocks all unrated sites once it is enabled, so it blocks thousands of perfectly innocent sites as well as the seedy ones. On the General tab of the Content Advisor dialog box, you can select an option to allow the display of unrated sites, but then you leave the gate open for the sites that are really offensive. Only you can decide on the best balance between information availability and protection.

Other censors

Several programs are available with more sophisticated censoring capabilities than those of the Content Advisor, which relies exclusively on ratings to screen content. CyberPatrol from Microsystems Software uses ratings but also allows users to develop lists of sites they want to avoid. SurfWatch from SurfWatch Software relies not on ratings but on a list of objectionable sites that it updates daily on its Web site. Filtering programs can be time-consuming to figure out and set up, and even the more sophisticated ones are not foolproof, so ongoing vigilance is necessary if you are determined to shield yourself or your family from objectionable material.

Other Ways
of Communicating

E-mail isn't the only way to communicate over the Internet. In this chapter, we show you how to communicate with specific people by using NetMeeting, and then we show you how to get your message out to the Web community by creating your own Web pages. We finish with a discussion of mailing lists.

Work together on one
document stored on
one computer

Type messages to
have an electronic
"conversation"

Send and receive
files and programs

Draw objects on a
collective whiteboard

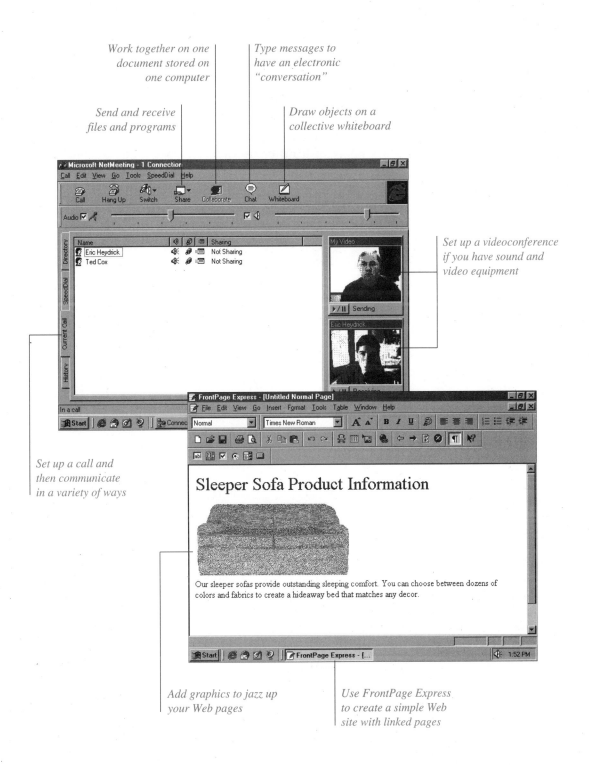

Set up a videoconference
if you have sound and
video equipment

Set up a call and
then communicate
in a variety of ways

Add graphics to jazz up
your Web pages

Use FrontPage Express
to create a simple Web
site with linked pages

Mastering e-mail is very important for efficient communication using the Internet, but with Internet Explorer 4 we can do much more than simply use e-mail to exchange short messages with colleagues and friends. In this chapter, we take a look at Internet communications of a different kind. First we explore some of the capabilities of the new Microsoft NetMeeting program. Then we show you how to communicate with the Web community at large by creating a simple Web page of your own. Finally we return to the topic of e-mail and discuss mailing lists (also known as *listservs*), a venerable Internet resource that still has its place in spite of all the new communication methods.

Using NetMeeting

Internet Explorer comes with the NetMeeting program, which supplements the written communication provided by Outlook Express with some exciting direct communication capabilities. With NetMeeting, we can *chat* with other people by typing what we want to say—they see what we type and we see what they type. And we can collaborate with others by working on a *whiteboard*—we can all see and manipulate whiteboard objects on our screens. NetMeeting also breaks new Internet ground in the realm of spoken and visual communications. If our computer is equipped with a sound card and microphone, we can hold *audioconferences* instead of placing long-distance telephone calls; and if our computer is equipped with a video camera and a video capture card, we can hold *videoconferences*. In this section, we'll briefly describe NetMeeting so that you can decide for yourself whether you want to take advantage of its capabilities.

Setting Up NetMeeting

Before we can use NetMeeting, we must set it up. Follow these steps:

1. Connect to your ISP and start Internet Explorer.

2. Choose Internet Call from the Go menu. The NetMeeting Setup Wizard starts and displays its introductory dialog box.

NetShow Player

Microsoft Internet Explorer 4 also includes a program called NetShow Player, used to access multimedia content across intranets and the Internet. To play *Active Streaming format* (.asf) files or to access live ASF streams, first point to the Start button, to Programs, to Internet Explorer, and then click NetShow Player. (ASF files are to ASF live streams as video tapes are to television broadcasts.) From the File menu, choose Open File to browse for .asf or .asx files in the Open dialog box, and double-click a file to play it. Or choose Open Location from the File menu, and type the URL or path to the file in the dialog box. Click OK to begin play. For more information about NetShow and NetShow Player, choose NetShow Home Page from the Go menu to visit that part of Microsoft's Web site.

3. Click Next to move to the next dialog box, which asks whether you want to log onto a directory server when you start Net-Meeting, so that you can see who is available to be contacted and other people can see you. The default directory server is *ils.microsoft.com*. (By the way, *ils* stands for *Internet locator server*.) This server will suit us for now, so click Next to move to this dialog box:

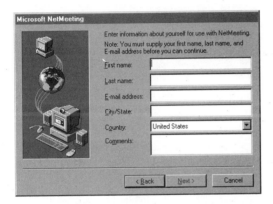

4. Enter your e-mail address and fill in any other boxes you wish. (This information appears in the directory listing, so think twice before divulging personal information.) Click Next to display this dialog box:

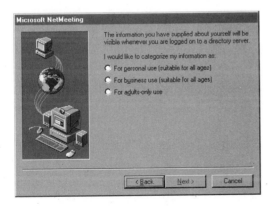

5. Select a category of use—for example, we selected For Business Use—and click Next.

6. The next step is to tune your audio settings by checking your voice. Follow the directions and when you're done, click

NetMeeting buttons not available

Many of the NetMeeting features we discuss in this chapter are available for use only if you are participating in a NetMeeting call. So if you can't find a particular button on the toolbar, it may be because you aren't yet participating in a call with at least one other NetMeeting user.

Finish to close the wizard and start NetMeeting. (If you don't have sound equipment on your computer, or you want to communicate with text only, follow the wizard's instructions and click Finish just as you would if you did have a sound card and microphone.)

7. If you see a message box that looks like this:

click OK and see the adjacent tip. A NetMeeting window like this one appears (we've maximized it):

The big difference between this window and others we've seen so far is that the viewing area is tabbed. At the moment, we are looking at the Directory tab, which tells us the category of NetMeeting use, the directory server to which we are logged on and information about all the other people logged onto this particular directory. (We'll look at some of the other tabs as we work our way through this section.)

8. To get ready for the next section, close NetMeeting, close Internet Explorer, and disconnect from your ISP.

Problems connecting to a directory server

Sometimes when you log onto NetMeeting, you might see a message box telling you of some sort of problem connecting to the default server. You can try to access a different server by clicking the arrow at the right end of the Server box on the Directory tab and selecting an option from the drop-down list. When you locate an available server, you can designate it as the one you want to log onto by choosing Options from the Tools menu, clicking the Calling tab, selecting the server from the Server Name drop-down list, and clicking OK. NetMeeting then attempts to log you onto that server. The new Server Name setting remains in effect as the default until you change it again.

Setting Up a Call

All NetMeeting activities take place in the context of a *call*. We first set up the call to establish contact with the person we want to communicate with and then indicate the type of communication we are going to use. As an example, suppose we want to "talk" to a colleague using NetMeeting. Here's how we would set up the call:

1. E-mail or phone the colleague and arrange for a NetMeeting call at a specific time and on a specific directory server. For this example, we have agreed to use *ils.business.four11.com* to talk.

2. At the designated time, connect to your ISP, start Internet Explorer, and then choose the Internet Call command from the Go menu to display the NetMeeting window shown on the previous page.

3. Choose Options from the Tools menu, and then on the Calling tab, set the Server Name setting to *ils.business.four11.com*. Click Yes when NetMeeting asks whether you want to log onto that server. After a pause, the list on the Directory tab refreshes itself to display information about the other people logged on. Anybody with a computer icon designated by a red asterisk is already involved in a call. A file transfer icon indicates the person is either using Chat or the Whiteboard, collaborating on a project, or sending files. A speaker icon indicates that the person's computer has sound equipment, and a camera icon indicates that his or her computer has video equipment.

4. Find the e-mail address of your colleague in the E-Mail column, right-click the listing, and choose Call from the object menu. The NetMeeting program on your computer contacts the NetMeeting program on your colleague's computer, asking whether he or she will accept the call. (This may take a while.) Once the call is accepted, the Current Call tab of the NetMeeting window becomes active and lists the call participants, as shown on the next page.

Switching to a different server

Receiving calls

By default, when someone asks whether you want to participate in a call, NetMeeting displays a dialog box with the name of the caller and gives you the option of accepting or rejecting the call. You can tell NetMeeting to automatically accept calls, by choosing Options from the Tools menu, and on the General tab, selecting the Automatically Accept Incoming Calls option. You can tell NetMeeting you don't want to be bothered by any calls by choosing the Do Not Disturb command from the Call menu.

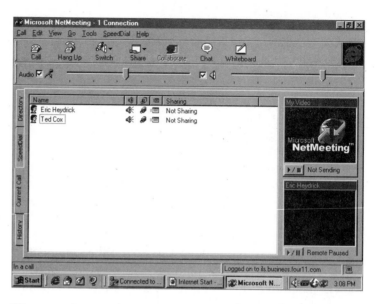

We can now communicate with call participants in a variety of ways, which we'll discuss in the next few sections. (When we are ready to end the call, we will simply click the Hang Up button on the NetMeeting toolbar.)

The Hang Up button

Chatting

Chatting is a relatively low-tech way of communicating by typing on the screen. It is popular because it's immediate, it's inexpensive, and unlike audio and videoconferencing, more than two people can get involved in the conversation. (Social chatting also offers the advantage of being anonymous; we can project a fantasy persona into cyberspace with very little risk that someone will call our bluff. Of course, the downside is that we never know whether the people we are "talking" to are also play-acting. The moral for those of you who want to use NetMeeting for socializing: have fun but be wary.) Assuming that you want to chat with the colleague with whom you've just established a call, follow these steps:

The Chat button

1. From the Current Call tab of the NetMeeting window, click the Chat button on the toolbar to display this Chat window:

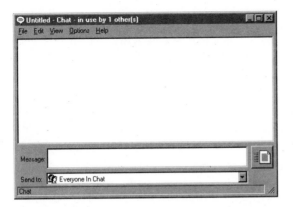

Clicking the Chat button automatically opens the Chat window on your colleague's screen as well as yours.

2. Type *When do you think you'll be finished with your review of the new specifications?* and press Enter. The message appears both on your screen and your colleague's. Here's what our screen looks like after a keyboard conversation:

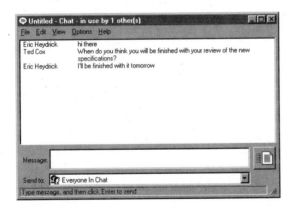

3. Click the Chat window's Close button to end the session, and when NetMeeting gives you the opportunity to save the conversation, click No.

We can save the conversation from a chat session at any time by choosing Save As from the File menu and assigning the chat file a name. Thereafter, we can save new versions of the same chat file by choosing the Save command. And we can print the conversation by choosing Print from the File menu.

Whispering

Suppose you are participating in a call with several other people and you want to chat with only one of them. You can select that person's name from the Send To drop-down list at the bottom of the Chat window, and when you type a message and press Enter, only that person will see what you typed.

Using the Whiteboard

Two or more call participants can work concurrently on projects by using NetMeeting's Whiteboard component. The Whiteboard is an onscreen drawing board, where we can collaboratively diagram processes, work out schedules, sketch designs, and so on. For this example, suppose we want to come to an agreement with a couple of colleagues based in distant cities about the procedure by which we will all write and produce a company report. We have already established a NetMeeting call and now we want to use the Whiteboard to diagram the procedure. Follow these steps:

The Whiteboard button

1. Click the Whiteboard button on the toolbar to display this Whiteboard window:

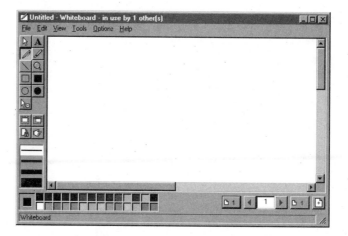

The Whiteboard automatically opens on the screens of all call participants when you send Whiteboard data to them. You can then capture parts of screens and place them on the Whiteboard using the commands at the bottom of the Tools menu; or you can copy items from other programs and paste them in from the Clipboard; or you can draw them from scratch.

The Unfilled Ellipse tool

2. Maximize the window, click the Unfilled Ellipse tool in the toolbox on the left side of the window, move to the top left corner of the window, hold down the left mouse button, and drag to draw a skinny oval.

The Text tool

3. Click the Text tool, click an insertion point at the left end of the oval, and type *Write* and your initials.

4. Continue to collaboratively draw ovals and lines to create a diagram that looks something like this:

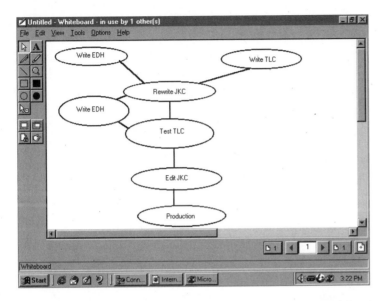

You can zoom in or out by choosing Zoom from the View menu or clicking the Zoom button.

The Zoom button

5. When you've finished, save the contents of the Whiteboard by choosing the Save As command from the File menu and assigning a filename.

6. Close the Whiteboard window.

We can also print out a paper copy of the Whiteboard's contents by choosing Print from the File menu.

Collaborating on Projects

Suppose we are working on a document and would like input from our colleagues. NetMeeting enables us to collaborate on such projects at two levels:

- **View only.** The owner of the document can share it with participants in a NetMeeting call in such a way that they can see the document but cannot work on it.

- **Change.** The owner can give other call participants access to the document so that they can make changes to it.

Collaborate with caution

When you collaborate with someone using NetMeeting, you are in effect giving that person access to your computer and its files. Obviously, you should be cautious about the people with whom you collaborate. If you share a Windows Explorer window, you share all windows that you open during that session, including any applications that you start while participating in the call. Sharing a folder on your computer shares all the subfolders, files and documents contained in that folder.

Let's go through the steps for both levels of collaboration using a hypothetical example. (In other words, you can't follow along with these steps, but the scenario will give you a good idea of how you might put this feature to work.)

1. Professor Oldham contacts, in advance, five of her Spanish students and five Spanish-speaking students from a variety of locations around the world. She tells them that she will be hosting a meeting (a call) on her computer at 7:15 PM, PDT, to enlist their help in producing the syllabus for a new Spanish Culture class that she will be teaching next semester. She makes sure they know her e-mail address and the ils directory she will use.

2. A few minutes before the specified time, Professor Oldham connects to her ISP, starts Internet Explorer, then starts Net-Meeting, and logs onto the specified directory.

Hosting a meeting →

3. She chooses Host Meeting from the Call menu and waits for the other participants to join her meeting.

4. The other participants start NetMeeting on their home, business, or school computers around the world and log onto the specified directory.

5. Assuming they already have a SpeedDial listing for Professor Oldham (see the tip below), they click the SpeedDial tab in the NetMeeting window and click Professor Oldham's entry to ask to join her meeting. As Professor Oldham accepts each participant, his or her name appears on the Current Call tab of everyone else's NetMeeting window.

Sorting the directory list

You can sort the directory list on any column by clicking its header. For example, click the E-Mail column header once to sort it alphabetically and click it again to reverse the sort order. You can also click the Audio or Video column header to group all the listings with audio or video.

SpeedDial

By default, NetMeeting adds the people you call and who call you to a list on the SpeedDial tab of its window. Click a name in the SpeedDial list to request a call with that person. To send your SpeedDial information, click the SpeedDial button on NetMeeting's toolbar, fill in the edit boxes, then click the Send To Mail Recipient option and click OK. (You can use this dialog box to manually add new SpeedDial information.) In the New Message window, enter the recipient's address and a Subject, and then send the message. Once people have your information in their SpeedDial list, all they have to do is click it to contact you.

6. Professor Oldham then clicks the Start button, chooses Microsoft Word from the Programs submenu, and opens a document called *Syllabus* on her computer.

7. She switches to NetMeeting and clicks the Share button on the NetMeeting toolbar. Then she switches back to Word and begins to work on the document. The call participants watch her work on the document, which appears in a window on their screens. Although they can't make any changes to the document, they can send their comments and suggestions to her by using Chat.

The Share button

8. Now Professor Oldham decides to let the call participants make changes to the Syllabus document. She flips over to NetMeeting, clicks the Collaborate button on the NetMeeting toolbar, and flips back to Word.

The Collaborate button

9. Any call participant who wants to take part in this collaborative endeavor also clicks the Collaborate button. He or she can click the mouse to take control of the cursor, and then insert and delete text in the usual way. (Obviously, only one person can edit the document at a time.)

10. When Professor Oldham decides she doesn't want any more assistance with the Syllabus document, she takes control of the document and stops the collaboration by pressing Esc (or clicking the Collaborate button again to deselect it).

Stopping collaboration

11. She ends the meeting by clicking the Hang Up button on the NetMeeting toolbar.

Sending and Receiving Files

Additionally, we can use NetMeeting's file sharing feature to send and receive files. Suppose that before terminating the call with her students, Professor Oldham decides all the call participants should have a copy of the Syllabus document. Here's how she would send the file to everyone:

1. Choose File Transfer and then Send File from the Tools menu to display the dialog box shown on the following page.

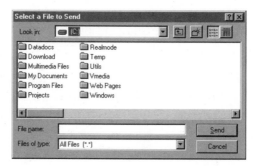

2. Browse for the file you want to send, select it, and click Open. (You can also drag the file onto the list of people on the Current Call tab.) The NetMeeting status bar indicates the progress of the file transfer.

3. When you see a message telling you the transfer was completed successfully, click OK.

   If we are on the receiving end of a file transfer, we see this dialog box when the transfer is complete:

We can then make a note of the name of the file and click OK. It will be stored in the C:\Program Files\NetMeeting\-Received Files folder.

Audioconferencing and Videoconferencing

Provided we have the necessary audio equipment, we can start a NetMeeting call and then carry on a conversation with one other audio-equipped participant by talking into a microphone and listening to responses over our speakers. And if we

Sending to one person

To send a file to only one of several call participants, right-click that person's name on the Current Call tab and choose Send File from the object menu. Then in the Open File dialog box, locate and double-click the file to start the transfer.

have the necessary video equipment, we can send and receive video images. Put the two together, and we can hold video-conferences (but the success of this experience will depend a lot on our equipment and server traffic). Here's how to participate in an audioconference or videoconference with a colleague:

1. Assuming you have started NetMeeting and are logged onto an agreed-upon directory server, locate the e-mail address of your colleague and request a call.

2. When the call is accepted, make sure that check marks appear in the microphone and speaker check boxes on the Audio toolbar, and then test the volume of your microphone and speakers by exchanging a few words of greeting. Make any necessary adjustments using the two volume control bars. (You can mute the microphone or the speakers by deselecting their check boxes.)

◄──────── *Audioconferencing*

3. Say what you need to say.

4. End the audio session (but not the call) by clicking the speaker icon next to the name of the person you are talking to on the Current Call tab and choosing Stop Using Audio And Video from the object menu.

5. Finally, end the call by clicking the Hang Up button on the NetMeeting toolbar.

Now let's try sending and receiving video images. We can send video images to a call participant who does not have video equipment attached to his or her computer, and we can also receive images whether or not we have video equipment. However, for this example, we will assume that both you and your colleague have the necessary cameras and video capture boards and that you're trying out this new means of communication. Follow these steps:

1. Before you set up a call, choose Options from the Tools menu and click the Video tab to display the options shown on the next page.

What do you look like?

If you want to check what you will look like to the person receiving your video image before you establish the call, click the button at the bottom of the My Video window. Check the lighting, your position in relation to the camera, and so on. When you're satisfied, place the call and proceed with the videoconference.

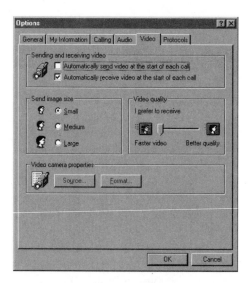

2. Select both the Automatically Send Video and Automatically Receive Video check boxes and click OK.

Videoconferencing

3. Back in the NetMeeting window, locate the e-mail address of the colleague with whom you want to exchange video data on the Directory tab and request a call. Assuming that both of you have selected the Automatically Receive Video and Automatically Send Video options, you can now see the call participant (or whatever images he or she is sending you) in the Remote Video window on the Current Call tab, like this:

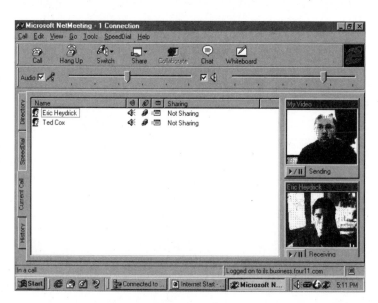

Video on demand

If you want to control when you send and receive video, you can deselect Automatically Send Video and Automatically Receive Video on the Video tab of the Options dialog box and then click the buttons at the bottom of the My Video and Remote Video windows to initiate the sending and receiving of video images.

4. When you've finished, end the video session by clicking the camera icon next to the name of the person you are communicating with on the Current Call tab and choosing Stop Using Audio And Video from the object menu.

5. Once again, end the call by clicking the Hang Up button on the NetMeeting toolbar.

You can start a call with several people and then talk to each of them in turn, or send video images to each in turn. Click the Switch button on the toolbar, select the name of the first person you want to communicate with, and talk and/or send video. Then click the Switch button, click the name of the second person, and talk and/or send video. And so on. While you are talking or sending video to one call participant, two other call participants can also be talking or sending video.

The Switch button

This has been a very quick overview of NetMeeting's capabilities—nothing more than a teaser, really. But if you frequently need to communicate with distant colleagues more directly than you can with e-mail (or regular mail), you might want to explore NetMeeting's capabilities further.

Creating Web Pages

As we explore the World Wide Web, we inevitably get ideas about ways we could use a Web site to communicate with potential customers about our product line, with existing customers about product availability and support, with colleagues about areas of professional interest, and so on. All we need is a design firm and a hefty budget for prototypes, roll-outs, and maintenance, right? It depends on the real purpose of the Web site and on how big a splash we want to make. If all we need is a simple, relatively static site that conveys the necessary information without much hoopla, we can take advantage of FrontPage Express, a stripped-down version of Microsoft's FrontPage Web authoring program, which is included with Internet Explorer 4. If nothing else, playing around with FrontPage will give you a feel for how Web sites are created and an appreciation for some of the more design-intensive sites you'll encounter on your Web excursions.

FrontPage Express

FrontPage Express is a WYSIWYG (What You See Is What You Get) program that enables you to design a Web page while viewing the results as they will appear in Internet Explorer. You no longer have to learn HTML coding to put together a decent-looking Web page. Although HTML is a logical coding system, it can be intimidating if you are not used to looking at coded documents. Here's an example:

1. Without connecting to your ISP, start Internet Explorer, which should display the Inter-Links file that was stored on your hard drive the last time you connected to the Internet.

Viewing the HTML source code

2. Choose Source from the View menu to display the HTML code for the Inter-Links home page in a Notepad window, like this:

```
Inter-Links.htm - Notepad
File  Edit  Search  Help
<HTML>
<HEAD>
    <TITLE>Inter-Links</TITLE>
</HEAD>
<!-- start header -->
<BODY BACKGROUND="background.gif" TEXT="#0000a0"
    LINK="#0800FF" ULINK="#F2000C">
<table width="100%" border="0" cellspacing="15"><tr>
<td valign="top">
<A HREF="toc.map">
<img border="0" src="toc.gif" alt=""  HEIGHT=335 WIDTH=1
<td><br>
<td valign="middle">
<center>
<H1>
<IMG SRC="new5.jpg" HEIGHT=264 WIDTH=344
```

3. Maximize the window and scroll the source document, marvelling at the complexity of the coding that displays the clean and simple Inter-Links home page in Internet Explorer. Believe it or not, some people can actually sit down and write this stuff, carrying in their heads an image of what all the coding will produce on the screen and checking the code in a browser from time to time to make sure the image is correct.

4. Click the Close button to close the Notepad window, and then close Internet Explorer.

Well, now that we've scared you, we'll show you the easy way to create a simple Web page. For our example, suppose we work for a company called Sofa City. We want to provide corporate information and advertise our products on the Web.

If you want to know more

Several sites on the Web provide information about HTML coding and Web page creation. If you're interested, you can take a look at the following sites:
http://sdcc8.ucsd.ed/~m1wilson/-htmlref.html
HTML Quick Reference
www.w3c.org/MarkUp/
W3C HTML resources
www.mcli.dist.maricopa.edu/tut/
Tutorial for writing HTML

Creating the Home Page

A Web site's home page is like the reception area of an office building. It announces who the owner is and communicates not only what the company or institution does but also its character. So the first thing to decide is whether we want to convey a polite and dignified handshake, a warm and folksy hug, or something in between. For the Sofa City example, we want a clean and simple, but friendly, look—some text and hyperlinks, but no animation or fancy effects. Follow these steps to see how we might get started:

1. Without connecting to your ISP, click the Start button, point to Programs, point to Internet Explorer, and choose FrontPage Express. You see this FrontPage Express window:

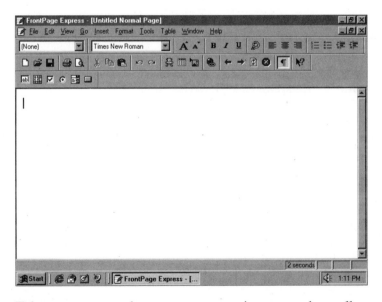

2. Take a moment to drag your mouse pointer over the toolbar buttons to learn their names and functions.

3. Start by typing a header at the top of the home page; for example, type *Sofa City*.

4. Center the header by selecting it and clicking the Center button on the toolbar. Then increase its size by clicking the Increase Text Size button a few times.

The Center and Increase Text Size buttons

5. Press End and then press Enter, and type a general statement about the company; for example, type *Sofa City is the leading retailer of quality sofas in the United States.*

The Decrease Text Size button

6. Select the sentence and reduce the size of the font by clicking the Decrease Text Size button. Then press End and Enter.

7. Insert a horizontal line to separate the header from the next section, by choosing Horizontal Line from the Insert menu.

8. Under the horizontal line, type *Our Guarantee* and format it as a centered header for this section.

9. Now type in some general statements about Sofa City's products; for example, type *Our sofas are made of only the highest quality materials. They are the most comfortable sofas you will ever sit on. No other sofa company can match our sofas for durability, design, and price.*

10. Insert another horizontal line under this section to set it off.

Now we'll create the section that provides links to pages of information about specific products. Follow these steps:

1. Type *About Our Products* and set off this header appropriately.

2. Next, type a general statement about getting product information and press Enter; for example, type *Click any of these hyperlinks for product information.*

The Bulleted List button

3. Now insert a bulleted list by clicking the Bulleted List button, typing the name of one type of sofa, and pressing Enter; for example, type *Sleeper Sofas.*

4. Continue typing bulleted items for other sofa types; for example, you might add *Leather Sofas, Casual Sofas, Formal Sofas.* When you're done, turn off the Bulleted List button.

5. Insert another horizontal line.

To finish off the home page, let's include ways customers can get in touch with the company:

1. Type *How to Reach Us* and format it as the section header.

2. Next, type a fictitious address and phone number.

3. Add a hyperlink to the company's e-mail address by clicking
the Create Or Edit Hyperlink button on the toolbar to display
this dialog box:

The Create Or Edit Hyperlink
button

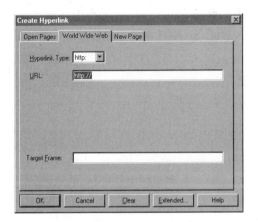

4. Click the arrow to the right of the Hyperlink Type box and
select Mailto. Then type // and a fictitious e-mail address in
the URL edit box and click OK. The FrontPage Express window now displays a hyperlink that is underlined, as it will be
when viewed in Internet Explorer.

Now let's put the final touches to the formatting of the page
and then save it:

1. Choose Background from the Format menu to display this
dialog box:

Changing background and
text colors

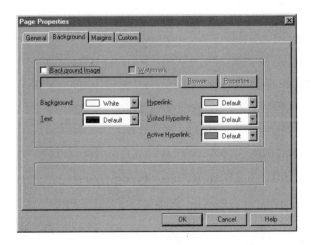

2. Select any color you want from the Background and Text drop-down boxes and click OK. (Make sure the text on the page is readable with your new color scheme.)

Saving the home page

3. Now choose Save As from the File menu and click the As File button in the Save As dialog box. Then create a new folder called *Website* on your hard drive, double-click the Website folder, type a name in the File Name box, and click Save.

Creating a Linked Page

We have finished creating Sofa City's home page. Now we'll turn our attention to one of the product pages and show you how to link two pages together. Follow these steps:

The New button

1. To start a blank page, click the New button on the toolbar.

2. Type and format a header for the page and press Enter; for example, type *Sleeper Sofa Product Information*.

3. Next, type some general statements about this type of sofa; for example, *Our sleeper sofas provide outstanding sleeping comfort. You can choose between dozens of colors and fabrics to create a hideaway bed that matches any decor.*

4. Suppose you want to insert a picture that is stored as a graphic file on your hard drive. Add it by choosing Image from the Insert menu, clicking the Browse button in the Image dialog box, and then double-clicking the image. For example, we inserted this picture of a sleeper sofa:

Formats for Web graphics

The pictures you insert on your Web pages must be in either GIF or JPEG format. If you have a picture you want to use but it is in a different format, you must convert it before inserting it in a Web page. If you are going to do any work with graphics for the Web, you should look into programs for graphics conversion and manipulation. For example, you can download Paint Shop Pro—a shareware program that enables you to easily convert one graphic format to another—from *www.jasc.com/psp.html*. After downloading, you can evaluate the program for 30 days before deciding whether to buy it.

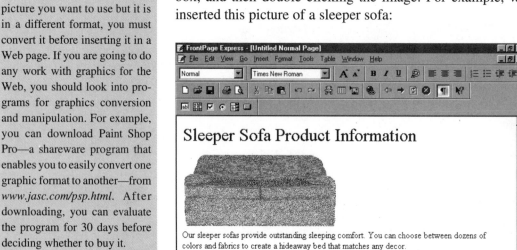

5. Save the product-information page in the Website folder.

Now we'll create the hyperlink from the home page to the product-information page. Follow these steps:

1. The home page is still open, so display it by choosing it from the Window menu.

2. In the About Our Products section, highlight *Sleeper Sofas* and click the Create Or Edit Hyperlink button on the toolbar to display the Create Hyperlink dialog box, which is shown on page 137.

3. Click the Open Pages tab, select the product-information page from the list, and click OK.

4. When FrontPage Express displays a message box telling you that you are creating a hyperlink to a local page, click Yes. Back on the home page, notice that Sleeper Sofas is now underlined as it will be in Internet Explorer.

5. Save the page and close FrontPage Express.

Viewing Web Pages in Internet Explorer

If we want to be sure that a Web site will look good and function correctly once it is out there on the Web, we can view the site's pages in Internet Explorer. Here's how:

1. Start Internet Explorer offline, type *c:\website* in the Address bar, and press Enter. You then see the contents of the Website folder displayed in the viewing area.

2. Double-click the home page file to display the Sofa City home page, and then click the *Sleeper Sofas* hyperlink to move to the product-information page, noticing that the path in the Address bar changes accordingly.

Obviously, the pages we have created are very simple, and they could be dramatically enhanced with graphics, colors, background images, video, and other elements. We will leave it up to you to explore on your own if you want to know more about creating Web pages.

The Web Publishing Wizard

After creating your Web site, you will want to publish it on the Internet. If you want your site to be available at any time, you must store the Web pages on a Web server with 24-hour access. (Most ISPs have hosting services for customers' pages.) You can use the Microsoft Web Publishing Wizard to transfer your Web pages to your ISP's Web server or to a Web server on your local area network (LAN). Before posting, you must start the Wizard by choosing it from the Internet Explorer submenu of the Start menu, and provide information about your Web server. When the Welcome dialog box appears, click New and add the requested information. Click Next and then Finish. To publish a single file or folder, start Microsoft Web Publishing Wizard and click Next when the Welcome dialog box appears. Click the Browse Folders or Browse Files button, select the folder or file you want to post, and click Open. Click Next, and in the Web Server box, click the drop-down arrow and select your Web server. (If your Web server does not appear in the drop-down list, click the New button to add it.) To publish multiple files to a Web server, open Windows Explorer and select the files you want to publish. Right-click the selected files, point to Send To, and choose Web Publishing Wizard. In the Web Server box, click the drop-down arrow and select your Web server. Click Next and then Finish.

Setting up a Web site

To set up a Web site so that is available on the Internet, we need access to a Web server. (See the tip on page 139 for more information.) Many ISPs provide space on their servers where account owners can post Web files, or we can investigate the many companies that provide this service for a monthly fee. The company we select to store our Web site will give us detailed instructions for sending the page files to their server and for updating the files as necessary.

Using Mailing Lists (Listservs)

Once we are proficient with e-mail, we might want to explore an e-mail based Internet resource known as *mailing lists*, or *listservs* (for *list servers*). They work like this: someone with a particular interest sets up a *mailing list server* for that topic and announces its availability to other people with the same interest. Those people e-mail the list server asking that their e-mail addresses be added to the topic's mailing list. They then send messages about the topic to the list server, and the server periodically forwards all the messages it receives to all the addresses on the list.

How they work

So how do we find out what mailing lists are available? As we browse the Internet, we'll come across references to lists, but here's a more direct approach:

1. Connect to your ISP, start Internet Explorer, and move to the Yahoo Web site.

2. Click Computers And Internet, then Internet, and then Mailing Lists. Scroll through the subject categories, checking out any that interest you. For example, we found car-related mailing lists by clicking on the Automotive category hyperlink.

3. When you've finished exploring, close Internet Explorer and disconnect from your ISP for the rest of this discussion.

When we find a mailing list that interests us, the next step is to subscribe to the list. The subscription procedure is usually spelled out in the mailing list's description and involves sending a message to the *subscription address* of a Listserv

A list of mailing lists

We recommend checking out Stephanie da Silva's Publicly Accessible Mailing Lists, an extensive list arranged hierarchically by topic, which is located at *www.neosoft.com/internet/paml*. If you think you might make use of mailing lists, you might want to add the URL for the Publicly Accessible Mailing Lists Web site to your favorites list.

program that administers the mailing list. The message follows a prescribed format, something like the following:

SUB <mailing-list> <Jill Doe>

where *<mailing-list>* and *<Jill Doe>* are placeholders for the name of the list and our name. When the program receives this message, it adds our e-mail address, which it gets from the header of the message, to its mailing list and sends a confirmation message with information about participating in the mailing list. We can send a message to the subscription address that says nothing but *HELP* to receive a list of other commands for working with the program. In the meantime, we can sit back and wait for the mailing list's messages to arrive.

To unsubscribe from the mailing list, we send a message like the following to the subscription address:

UNSUB <mailing-list> <Jane Doe>

After subscribing to a mailing list, we don't have to do anything to receive its messages. They will show up in our Inbox along with our e-mail. Before sending any messages to a mailing list, it's best to read the incoming messages for a while, to get an idea of the kinds of topics being discussed and the format and tone being used. (See page 160 for more information about the etiquette of public-forum participation.)

Receiving and sending messages

When we are ready, we can start a new discussion by clicking the To: Mail button on the toolbar, entering the *list address* of the mailing list, typing our message, and sending it on its way. If we want to contribute to an ongoing discussion, we should first decide whether the entire mailing list will benefit from our words of wisdom or whether we should respond directly to the author of a message rather than take up the time of everyone on the list. Based on this decision, we can click the Reply To Author or Reply To All button on the toolbar, check the To box to make sure our message is going to the correct destination, and then compose and send our message in the usual way.

We'll leave you on your own to check out mailing lists further while we move on to a discussion of newsgroups.

Mailing-list restraint

It is tempting to subscribe to lots of mailing lists, thinking that we should take as much advantage as possible of all the freely available information. But be warned: subscribing to a few active mailing lists can completely swamp your Inbox. Select mailing lists carefully, subscribing to them one at a time. Rigorously test them for relevancy, and unsubscribe immediately if they are not providing needed information.

6
Participating in Newsgroups

We use Outlook Express to show you how to find Usenet newsgroups that match your interests, how to subscribe to those you want to visit regularly, and how to select and read articles. Then we demonstrate ways to post and follow up on articles.

*Subscribe to the
newsgroups you want
to participate in*

*Post articles and follow-ups
using the Compose Message
and Reply To Group buttons*

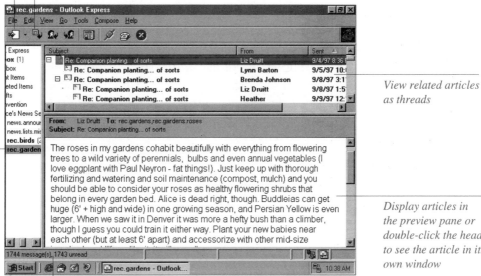

*View related articles
as threads*

*Display articles in
the preview pane or
double-click the header
to see the article in its
own window*

*Download all the
articles in a newsgroup
to catch up on the
current discussions*

What are newsgroups?

Newsgroups and *network news* are terms used to refer to a vast collection of public discussion groups, organized around literally thousands of topics, that are accessible via the Internet. (They are also accessible in other ways, but we won't go into that here.) Newsgroups are the closest thing the Internet has to a community bulletin board, where we can check out the latest messages about a mind-boggling number of subjects. We can passively read these messages or actively participate in a discussion by contributing our own messages in a way that is very similar to sending e-mail. As active participants, we can ask questions, help resolve other people's problems, gossip, rave about a hero, debate a Supreme Court decision, exchange recipes, get automobile recommendations, research any subject that is dear to our wallets or our hearts, and generally while away many an hour interacting with others who share our interests or needs.

In this chapter, we show you how to use the *news reader* component of Outlook Express to join a couple of the online conversations that are available through Usenet, the largest of the newsgroup systems. We discuss how to determine which newsgroups are likely to focus on topics that interest you and which ones are most likely to cater to "fringe" tastes. We show you how to join a newsgroup gracefully and how to become a valued member of the groups where you decide to concentrate your time.

Newsgroups vs. mailing lists

The difference between these two Internet resources lies in their delivery methods. With a mailing list, copies of the messages on the list are made for each subscriber and are sent to his or her mailbox. (See page 140 for information about mailing lists.) With a newsgroup, a copy of the group's articles is stored on each news server and the subscribers make their own copies of articles only if they want to keep them.

Newsgroup Concepts

Internet service providers can use one of their servers to carry all or some of the Usenet newsgroups, and many ISPs will carry other newsgroups as well, including regional newsgroups that cater to local interests. However, some ISPs don't carry newsgroups at all. As long as your ISP has a news server, you can tap into this huge reservoir of information and social interaction without any additional software. Outlook Express includes the *Network News Transfer Protocol* (or *NNTP*) needed to participate in newsgroups, as well as the necessary protocols to send and receive e-mail messages.

So how do newsgroups operate? Suppose we work for a mail-order company that sells gardening and yard products. Part of our job is to research trends that affect the company's target market, so we want to participate in newsgroups frequented by gardeners and other people who might use our products. We connect to our ISP, start Outlook Express, and select an appropriate newsgroup, where we can read any relevant messages, called *articles*, that other people have already contributed. When we are ready to become an active participant, we can *post* new articles and *follow up* on articles posted by others.

← How newsgroups work

← Articles

← Posting and following up

Newsgroups are usually organized hierarchically by topic (see the next section for more information). Most newsgroups are *unmoderated*, meaning that they allow anyone to post or follow up on articles. Some are *moderated*, meaning that they require that all submissions—both new articles and follow-ups—be sent to the group's moderator for approval. The moderator then posts those that he or she feels are relevant and useful. Articles within newsgroups are organized into clusters, called *threads*, that consist of the original article and any follow-ups. So instead of reading newsgroups chronologically, we read subject-based threads that may have evolved over several days or even weeks as various people added their two cents.

← Unmoderated vs. moderated newsgroups

← Threads

Newsgroup Hierarchies

The more traditional newsgroups are organized into categories, which are divided into subcategories, which are in turn divided into sub-subcategories, and so on. Their names follow this hierarchy, identifying first the category, then the subcategory, and then the sub-subcategory, with each level separated from the next by a period. Sound confusing? Here's a typical Usenet newsgroup name:

misc.education.home-school

Reading from left to right, the general category is *misc* (for *miscellaneous*), the subcategory is *education*, and the sub-subcategory is *home-school*.

About Usenet

Like the Internet, Usenet is not a *thing*, but it's not a *network*, either. It's a loose association of news administrators who allow their servers to function as Usenet distribution sites, called *newsfeeds*.

Because ISPs can decide which newsgroups to carry on their servers, not all providers carry all available groups. So that we can be reasonably sure you will have access to the newsgroups used in our examples, we focus on Usenet newsgroups, which are divided into general categories like these:

Primary Usenet categories →

biz	Business (commercial)
comp	Computer-related
K12	Teaching and students
misc	Miscellaneous topics
news	Usenet information
rec	Recreation and leisure activities
sci	Science (except for computer science, which is in *comp*)
soc	Social issues and all kinds of socializing
talk	Topic-based, often heated discussions

You might also have access to the catch-all *alt* (for *alternative*) category of Usenet newsgroups, which includes everything that doesn't fit into the other categories, including lifestyle groups and pornography posing as art (or simply posing!). We'll talk more about the significance of newsgroup hierarchies as we work with Outlook Express, but first, we have one procedural step to take care of.

Setting Up Outlook Express for News

If you work for a large organization or you access the Internet through a school computer, your computer has probably already been set up to access newsgroups. If that is the case, you can skip this section and jump to page 150, where we tell you how to browse through the available newsgroups. If newsgroup access is not yet set up on your computer, you need to tell Outlook Express the domain name of the server that handles newsgroups and some information about yourself. Assuming that you have already completed the steps for setting up Outlook Express for e-mail (see page 69), follow these steps:

1. Obtain the domain name of your news server from your ISP.

2. Connect to your ISP and start Outlook Express.

Blocking newsgroups

If you want to be able to browse through newsgroups without being confronted by smutty articles, you can use a filtering program to block the display of any newsgroup containing this type of material. Programs such as CyberPatrol and SurfWatch come with regularly updated databases of offending Web sites, newsgroups, FTP servers, and Gopher servers; and they work by simply hiding anything in the database from view.

3. Click Outlook Express in the left pane to display these options in the right pane:

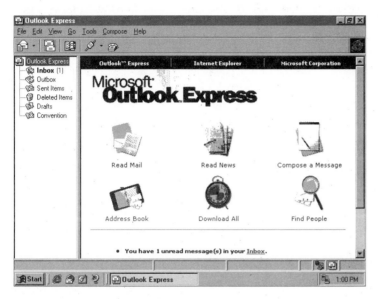

4. Click Read News in the right pane to start the Internet Connection Wizard, which displays this dialog box:

Setting news options

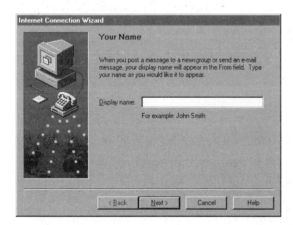

5. Enter the requested information, clicking the Next button to move from one dialog box to the next. You will need to enter the following:

- Your first and last name (for example, *Jill Doe*)

- Your full Internet e-mail address (for example, *jdoe@hal-cyon.com*)

- The name of your news (NNTP) server (for example, *news.-halcyon.com*). If your ISP requires you to log in to the news server, click the check box at the bottom of this dialog box.

- A friendly name that Outlook Express will use for your news settings (for example, *Jill Doe's News Settings*)

- Your Internet connection type (if you use a modem to connect to your ISP, select Connect Using My Phone Line; otherwise, select Connect Using My Local Area Network)

6. In the wizard's last dialog box, click Finish to save your news settings. You then see this dialog box:

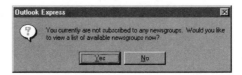

7. Click No to close the dialog box, then close Outlook Express and, if necessary, disconnect from your ISP.

Exploring Usenet Newsgroups

For efficiency, every Usenet user should read a few specific newsgroups before setting off on broader exploration. The *news* newsgroups category offers a wealth of information about how to get started with newsgroups, as well as some interesting historical Usenet background. We strongly recommend that you read the articles in the *news.answers* and *news.announce.newusers* groups before you post any articles of your own, and we show you in a moment how to save these articles on your hard disk as files so that you can read them offline. These articles were written by newsgroup veterans and offer sound advice on how to participate in newsgroups. (They reinforce the information we provide in this chapter.) We don't recommend that you read the articles in the *news.newusers.questions* newsgroup. Often these articles are posted by people who haven't taken the time to read *news.announce.newusers* and *news.answers* articles, and who can't wait to post something—*anything*—to a newsgroup. At any point in time, this group might contain a few thousand

Read these

Don't read these

articles, most of which either ask questions already answered by articles in the other two *news* newsgroups—a big no-no—or ask questions that should be posted in a different newsgroup—an even bigger no-no. Other articles are presumably someone's idea of a joke or someone's attempt at being risqué or downright shocking. At best they are immature, and at worst they are offensive. The only use we have found for the articles in this newsgroup is that they provide examples of what *not* to do in other newsgroups if you want to avoid the scorn of the Usenet community.

Having given you a taste of what to expect, let's start exploring. Follow these steps:

1. Connect to your ISP and start Outlook Express.

2. Click your news settings entry in the left pane of the Outlook Express window or choose the News command from the Go menu. Outlook Express displays the dialog box shown on the facing page, asking whether you want to view a list of the newsgroups available from your news server.

◄─────── Displaying the newsgroup list

3. Click Yes. Downloading the entire list of groups can take some time, depending on the number of available groups and your connection speed. Once the list of groups is downloaded and saved in a file on your hard drive, you see this Newsgroups dialog box:

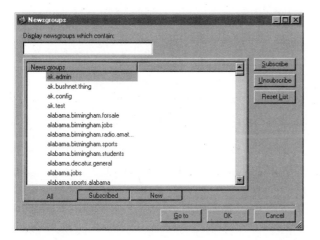

We select the newsgroups we want to read and subscribe to in this dialog box. Selecting a newsgroup and then clicking the Go To button at the bottom of the dialog box downloads the newsgroup's articles and displays them in the Outlook Express window. In the next section, we find out what newsgroups are available and show you how to move around.

Browsing Newsgroups

As we said, the *news* newsgroups are a good place for newcomers to get their feet wet. Let's take a look at some of the articles in the *news.announce.newusers* group. (If this group is not available, use *news.answers* instead.) Try this:

Narrowing down the list

1. Type *news* in the Display Newsgroups Which Contain edit box. Now the list box shows only the newsgroups that contain the word *news* in their names.

Displaying newsgroup contents

2. Scroll the list box until you see *news.announce.newusers,* select it, and click the Go To button. Outlook Express retrieves about 300 of the group's articles from your news server and displays their headers in the top right pane of the Outlook Express window. (This may take a while.)

3. Display more of the article headers by dragging the borders of the panes so that the window looks something like this:

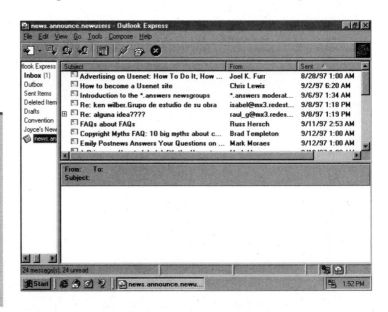

About the *.answers newsgroups

When you first check out the contents of a newsgroup, we recommend that you look for an answers subcategory to find out what the newsgroup traditionally covers and what the rules for participation are. (All the *.answers* articles should also be posted in *news.answers.*)

In the top right pane is the subject, the sender's name, the date and time the article was posted and (out of view) the size of the message. When we have not yet read an article, the header is displayed in bold type. By the way, the list of articles on your screen will be different from ours because the articles in newsgroups change constantly. ISPs set expiration policies that range from one day to a few weeks for each newsgroup, and articles are automatically removed according to those expiration policies. Because the *news.announce.newusers* newsgroup is an important reservoir of basic information about Usenet, its articles are regularly reposted to the newsgroup to keep them available. Even so, your list won't be exactly the same as ours. (The articles you'll see in the other newsgroups we'll visit will also vary from those on our screens.)

◄——— **Expiring articles**

4. Scroll the headers in the top pane, noticing that some articles answer frequently asked questions (FAQs) about specific newsgroups and some provide more general information.

5. In the top pane, click an article header, such as *Answers to Frequently Asked Questions about Usenet*. Outlook Express displays the article in the preview pane with a header bar, much like an e-mail message header, across the top.

◄——— **Displaying articles**

6. Enlarge the preview pane by dragging its top border up, and scroll the article to see its information, like this:

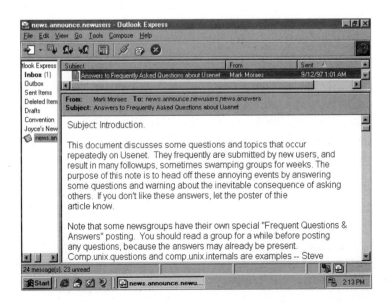

Saving Articles to Read Offline

The *Answers* article is pretty long, and we don't want to spend time reading it online. We could choose Print from the File menu to print the article, but we don't really need a paper copy. Instead, let's save the article as a file so that we can read it later. (If you clicked a different article, save it instead.)

1. With the *Answers to Frequently Asked Questions about Usenet* article displayed in the preview pane of the Outlook Express window, choose Save As from the File menu.

2. Type A*nswers* as the file name, change the Save As Type setting to Text Files, create a folder called News Articles in a convenient place on your hard drive, move to that folder, and click Save to save the file.

Now we can read the article at our leisure by opening it in any word-processing program. We suggest you glance through all the headers in *news.announce.newusers* and *news.answers* and save and then read the articles you're interested in.

Exploring Other Available Newsgroups

Having practiced with the *news* newsgroups, let's take a look at some other newsgroups that are available:

The News Groups button

1. Click the News Groups button on the toolbar to open the Newsgroups dialog box shown earlier on page 149.

2. Scroll the groups list so that you can see the abundance of newsgroups.

Searching newsgroups with DejaNews

One of the search tools available to you from the Internet Start page is DejaNews, which you can use to search newsgroups for a particular topic. For example, if you enter the keyword *potatoes*, Deja-News produces more than 2700 articles in newsgroups as diverse as *rec.food.cooking*, *alt.music.-queen*, and *sci.med.nutrition*.

3. Scroll to the *news.lists.misc* newsgroup, select it, and then click the Go To button. Outlook Express retrieves this group's articles from your news server. Each article preceded by a plus sign has hidden follow-up articles about the same topic, and the entire group is a thread.

4. Click the plus sign located to the left of *List Of Periodic Informational Postings* to display all the articles in this thread. Notice that the lower-level articles are indented under the top-level article.

5. Adjust the panes' sizes and then click the header of one of the *List of Periodic Informational Postings* articles to display the article in the preview pane.

6. Scroll the article to see its contents, which resemble these:

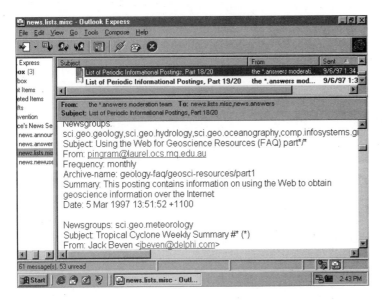

All the *Informational Postings* articles follow this format. They list, alphabetically, the Usenet newsgroups that provide FAQs or other information about themselves. With so many newsgroups to choose from, it's hard to find those that cover topics we're interested in. The *Informational Postings* articles are one place to start looking. These and other articles found in the *news* newsgroup can shed some light on the structure of the Usenet newsgroups so that we can start looking for what we need in the primary Usenet categories (see the list on page 146). We'll leave it to you to check out any other newsgroups available through your ISP.

Subscribing to Newsgroups

When we find a newsgroup we want to participate in, or at least check regularly for new articles, we can *subscribe* to that newsgroup. Don't worry: subscribing doesn't mean you have to fork over any money. As with Web sites, we subscribe to a newsgroup to tell Outlook Express that we have more than

Newsgroup acronyms

Here are some of the acronyms used most frequently by newsgroup participants:

BTW	By the way
IMHO	In my humble opinion
OTOH	On the other hand
ROTFL	Rolling on the floor, laughing
RTFM	Read the *fill-in-the-blank* manual
WRT	With respect to
YMMV	Your mileage (experience) may vary

a passing interest in it. We can then display only the newsgroups to which we have subscribed.

As a demonstration of how to subscribe to a newsgroup, we'll use the garden and yard products mail-order company we mentioned as an example on page 145. First we need to find a newsgroup frequented by gardeners:

Finding newsgroups →

1. Although some people make their living as professional gardeners, for the majority of people, gardening is a hobby. So start by clicking the News Groups button to open the Newsgroups dialog box, and then scrolling the list of newsgroups until you see the *rec.gardens* (for *recreation.gardens*) newsgroup. (Or you can type *gardens* in the Display Newsgroups Which Contain edit box to narrow the groups list.)

2. The *rec.gardens* newsgroup has a few sub-subcategories, but you're interested in general gardening issues. So click the *rec.gardens* newsgroup to select it and click the Subscribe button on the right to subscribe. Outlook Express displays an icon next to the group name, and the dialog box now looks something like this:

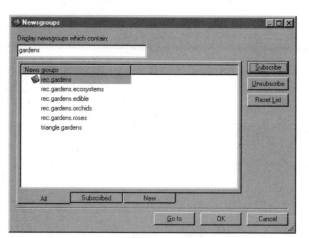

Filtering articles

Once you get to know a newsgroup and its regular participants, you can apply filters that will ensure that articles matching criteria you specify are not displayed. Choose Newsgroup Filters from the Tools menu, click Add, select the newsgroup you want to filter, specify the criteria for filtering, and click OK.

Now we'll subscribe to a couple of other likely sources of related backyard information and display only the subscribed groups. Follow these steps:

1. In the Newsgroups dialog box, scroll the list of groups to locate *rec.birds,* select it, and click the Subscribe button. (If

you typed *gardens* in the edit box, double-click it to select it
and press Delete to redisplay the entire list. Then you can type
rec. or *birds* to narrow the list again.)

2. Next, subscribe to *talk.environment*.

3. Click the Subscribed tab in the Newsgroups dialog box and,
   if necessary, delete the entry in the edit box to display these
   results:

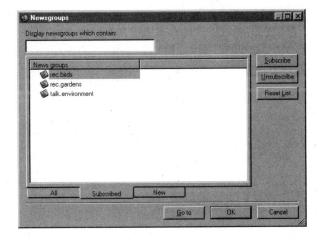

For demonstration purposes, we might as well show you how
to unsubscribe from a newsgroup. Try this:

1. On the Subscribed tab of the Newsgroups dialog box, select
   the *talk.environment* newsgroup and click the Unsubscribe
   button. Outlook Express removes its icon.

2. Click OK to close the dialog box.

Controlling the Display of Articles

Let's check out a few of the articles in the *rec.gardens*
newsgroup:

1. Click *rec.gardens* in the left pane to display its articles in the
   top right pane, and then click the first article in the right pane
   to display its text in the preview pane, as shown at the top of
   the next page. (As with e-mail messages, you can double-click
   an article header to display the article in its own window.)

Unsubscribing

Checking the numbers

If you click your news settings
entry in the left pane, Outlook
Express displays in the right pane
a list of subscribed newsgroups
with the total number of articles
and the number you have not read.
From this information you can
judge whether to display a newsgroup's articles. If you keep up
with the articles in a subscribed
newsgroup, you can tell whether
anything new has been posted
since your last visit just by looking at this list.

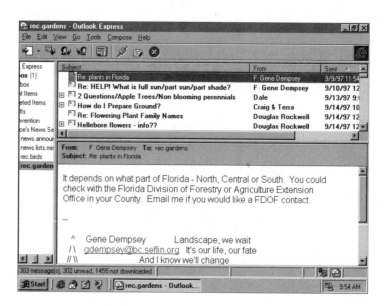

As you have seen, when we read an article in a newsgroup, Outlook Express indicates that the article has been read by changing its type. Notice also that the number of articles listed, the number of articles that are unread, and the number available but not yet downloaded are displayed in the Outlook Express status bar. The *rec.gardens* newsgroup members are a very active bunch!

2. Scroll through the list in the top pane, clicking the headers of any articles of interest.

By default, Outlook Express downloads and displays the headers of the 300 newest articles. Suppose you have read these messages and you now want to see others that you haven't read. Here's what you do:

1. Click the headers of a dozen or so articles that don't have plus signs beside them, pausing long enough on each one for it to change from bold to regular type.

2. Choose Current View and then Unread Messages from the View menu.

3. Now scroll the list of articles, noticing that all those you clicked in step 1 have now disappeared from the list.

Getting a handle on large newsgroups

When you first start reading a newsgroup, the number of articles can seem overwhelming. To start with, you might want to mark all the articles as read by choosing the Mark All As Read command from the Edit menu. Then you can read all new articles posted from today on, without feeling compelled to go back and read existing articles. (Usenet wisdom has it that anything worth discussing will come up again, and you can catch it next time around.)

4. Repeat step 1 for the next several *rec.gardens* articles.

5. Now click *rec.birds* in the left pane and then click *rec.gardens* again. The headers for the articles you clicked in step 4 have disappeared from the top right pane.

6. To retrieve more articles, choose Download This Newsgroup from the Tools menu to display this dialog box:

Downloading all the articles for a newsgroup

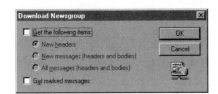

7. Select the Get The Following Items option, and with New Headers selected, click OK. Outlook Express then downloads the headers for the remaining articles in the *rec.gardens* newsgroup.

   As you scrolled through the list of *rec.gardens* articles, you probably noticed all the threads indicated by plus signs. Let's read a thread:

1. Click the plus sign preceding a thread that does not begin with *Re:*, such as the one shown here:

Reading threads

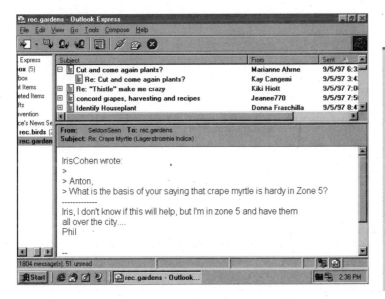

Downloading more articles

Outlook Express can retrieve a maximum of 1000 articles at a time. When you display a newsgroup, by default the program retrieves about 300 articles. To increase this number, choose Options from the Tools menu and on the Read tab, change the setting in the Download box. Alternatively, you can choose Get Next 300 Headers from the Tools menu to see 300 new articles at a time.

The *Re:* in the header of the indented article indicates that it is a response to the top-level article.

2. Click the plus sign preceding the header of a thread that does begin with *Re:*. For example, we clicked the plus sign preceding the *Re: Companion planting* thread and then selected the top-level article shown here:

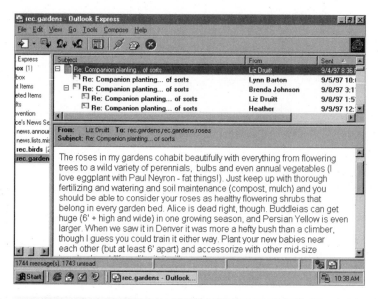

The *Re:* in the top-level header indicates that this article and those that are indented under it are responses to an earlier article that is no longer part of the thread because it has expired (see page 151).

3. Click one of the lower-level articles in the thread to display it in the preview pane.

Marking a thread as read → 4. You've read enough of this thread to know that it's of no interest to you, so choose Mark Thread As Read from the Edit menu. The entire thread is marked as read, even though you displayed only a couple of its articles.

Suppose we have read all the articles and we want to follow up on some of them, so we don't want "read" articles to be removed if we switch to another group. Follow the steps on the facing page.

1. Choose Current View and then All Messages from the View menu and press Ctrl+Home to move to the first header in the top right pane. The read articles reappear.

Displaying all articles

2. Choose Mark All As Read from the Edit menu to mark the entire newsgroup as read.

Marking all articles as read

OK, so now all the messages are displayed and they are all marked as read. But how do you identify those you want to follow up on? You can mark them as unread so that only they appear in the list in bold type, and you can then jump from unread message to unread message. Try this:

1. Choose Sort By and then Ascending from the View menu to turn off ascending sort order and show the most recent articles first in the top right pane.

2. Click the header of an article in order to display its text in the preview pane.

3. Choose Mark As Unread from the Edit menu.

4. Repeat steps 2 and 3 to mark a few more articles as unread.

5. Now press Ctrl+Home to move to the top of the list, and choose Next and then Next Unread Message from the View menu to jump to the first "unread" article.

6. Press Ctrl+U to jump to the second unread article.

7. With the article displayed in the preview pane and without quitting Outlook Express, disconnect from your ISP. (You shouldn't be connected for the rest of this chapter.)

Having read a few articles contributed by others, let's see how you might contribute some of your own.

Posting Articles

The procedure for posting articles to a newsgroup is relatively simple. The etiquette involved can be another matter, depending on the nature of the newsgroup we want to post in. Some newsgroups are inflammatory and nothing we can say will turn up the heat any higher. Others are informal and forgiving

Other ways of sorting

As you'll see if you choose Sort By from the View menu, articles are sorted by thread (so that the articles that belong to a thread appear together no matter when they were sent) and then by the date they were sent. You won't want to change the Group Messages By Thread setting, but you might want to sort the articles by subject or by sender. Experiment with different sort orders to see which work best for you.

of the mistakes *newbies* (new users) can make. But the most informative and useful newsgroups are often those that have been around for a while and whose participants get irritated when newcomers barge in without bothering to learn their rules. These rules are perfectly reasonable and are designed to avoid wasting everyone's time, so bear them in mind:

- Read the newsgroup's FAQ if it has one (for Usenet newsgroups, look in *news.answers* or in the category's *.answers* newsgroup). You may have noticed that the FAQs described in the *Informational Postings* articles (see page 152) often mention in their summaries that they are required reading for anyone wanting to post an article to that particular newsgroup. Take these requirements seriously if you want to be taken seriously by the group.

- Read the newsgroup's existing articles to get a feel for the kinds of issues the newsgroup deals with. If you're burning to ask a question or bring up an issue that doesn't fit the pattern, look somewhere else. Off-topic articles can provoke strident follow-ups.

- Also read the articles to make sure someone hasn't already asked your question or put your issue on the table for discussion. That means *all* the articles. Outlook Express only downloads a certain number of articles at a time (see page 157), so choose Get Next 300 Headers from the Tools menu until you have read them all.

The main point to remember is that every article we post takes up time for the newsgroup's readers and takes up disk space on the thousands of news servers that are the backbone of the newsgroup system. Tossing a casual contribution into a newsgroup as we whiz by may seem harmless enough, but why bother if we don't intend to return to see people's responses? The value of a newsgroup depends on the quality of the ideas and information exchanged over time or on the fun people have communicating electronically with each other. If you spend much time in a newsgroup, you'll find that you get out of it only as much as you put into it, and pretty soon, you'll get as irritated by casual intruders as the veteran members do.

Efficient browsing

You can increase your efficiency with newsgroups by working offline as much as possible. To set up a newsgroup so that you can browse its headers offline, right-click the newsgroup in the left pane and choose Properties from the object menu. On the Download tab, first click the When Downloading option and then select New Headers and click OK. You then download only the headers of new articles posted to the group. Offline, you can browse through the headers, select an article of interest, and then choose Mark For Retrieval and Mark Message from the Tools menu. Then connect to your ISP and choose Download All from the Tools menu to download the articles whose headers you have marked. If you want to work online, you can browse and mark headers by first choosing Options from the Tools menu, clicking the Read tab, deselecting the Automatically Show News Messages In The Preview Pane option and clicking OK. To read a particular article, select its header and press the Spacebar.

Well, that's enough preaching. It's time to see how to post articles. In the following sections, you aren't connected to your ISP, so you can't actually post. But our descriptions will give enough information for you to be able to post your own articles later on.

Following Up on Articles

Suppose we want to follow up on the article whose text is now displayed in the bottom right pane of the Outlook Express window. Follow these steps:

1. Click the Reply To Group button on the toolbar to display this window:

The Reply To Group button

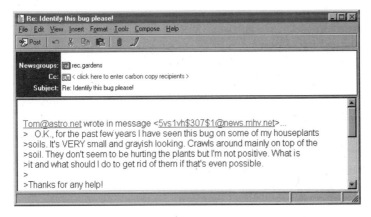

Notice that the Newsgroups and Subject boxes are already filled in. The subject is the same as that of the article you are following up on, with *Re:* added if the original article is the start of a thread. If this article has already been stored on your hard drive, or if you are connected to your ISP, the original article appears at the bottom of the message area preceded by > marks. You can edit this quoted material as appropriate.

2. For demonstration purposes, type a short, courteous reply and choose Send Later from the File menu. Depending on the length of the article and of your reply, you might see the dialog box on the next page.

Sending to the Outbox

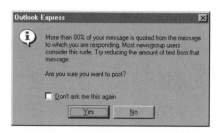

3. In this case, you can simply click Yes.

The Post button

That's it! Under normal circumstances, we would be connected to our ISP and could click the Post button on the toolbar to send the follow-up on its way. As it is, Outlook Express puts the article in the Outbox, waiting for the next time we connect to the Internet.

Posting New Articles

Composing and posting new articles is similar to composing and sending e-mail messages except that we don't have to enter the address of the recipient. Follow these steps:

The Compose Message button

1. With the *rec.gardens* newsgroup still active in the left pane of the Outlook Express window, click the Compose Message button to open a window with the newsgroup's name already in the Newsgroups box.

2. Type a subject, press Tab, and type an article like this one:

E-mailing a follow-up

Sometimes it is more appropriate to e-mail a response to the person who posted an article than it is to take up the time of newsgroup members with a follow-up, especially if the response contributes little to the general discussion. (A *thank you* note falls into this category.) You can click the Reply To Author button to send an e-mail response. You can click the Forward Message button to forward an article via e-mail to a specific person.

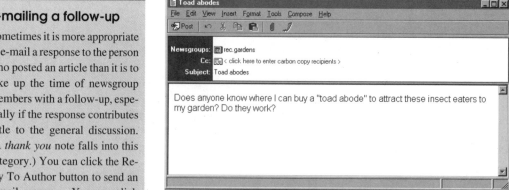

3. Because you are not connected to your ISP, choose Send Later from the File menu to simulate posting the article. (Again, you click the Post button when you are posting real articles.)

4. When a message appears telling you the article will be placed in your Outbox, click OK.

If we were actually posting this article, it would show up in the newsgroup after a while as the beginning of a new thread. Other people's follow-ups would be given *Re:* headers and be grouped under our article to designate them as responses, whether they were posted hours or even days later.

We have one bit of tidying up to do before we end this chapter. We used the Send Later command, so our articles are now sitting in Outlook Express's Outbox and we need to delete them:

1. Click the Outbox in the left pane of the Outlook Express window to display its two items in the top right pane:

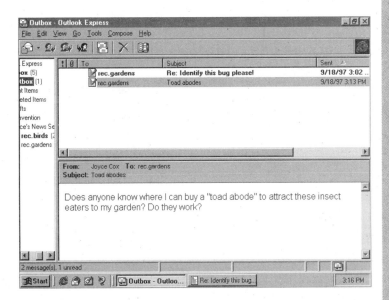

2. Select both articles and click the Delete button on the toolbar. Now there's no chance that your bogus articles will waste the time of the *rec.gardens* members.

3. Close Outlook Express.

You are now equipped to integrate the Internet into your daily life, and we'll leave you to continue exploring its constant evolution.

Advertising

Commercial advertising is really frowned on in most newsgroups and is likely to instigate flaming (as well as boycotts). *Spamming* (the practice of posting the same material to multiple newsgroups) is virulently opposed, not only by newsgroup members themselves but also by ISPs, who have been known to cancel the accounts of people caught in the act. Some newsgroups tolerate a simple, non-hyped announcement of a new product or service that directly relates to the members' interests. Such announcements are less likely to raise hackles if they come from a seasoned member with a reputation for intelligent participation in the newsgroup; in other words, don't just drop in on a newsgroup and make an announcement. Some categories have want-ad or marketplace subcategories for personal, not commercial, transactions. The usefulness of these newsgroups is limited, however, because not many people will buy used merchandise without seeing and testing it.

Index